Phyllis Wheatley

Slave and Poet

Gerald W. Morton

PublishAmerica
Baltimore

First printing

PublishAmerica has allowed this work to remain exactly as the author intended, verbatim, without editorial input.

ISBN: 1-60474-855-9
PUBLISHED BY PUBLISHAMERICA, LLLP
www.publishamerica.com
Baltimore

Printed in the United States of America

Dedication

To the memory of Florence Thomas

Chapter I

A Child Abducted

"That child, John. Look at her," Susanna Wheatley said as she and her husband walked along the docks at the Beach Street Wharf of Boston Harbor. There Massachusetts businessman John Avery was selling approximately 75 newly-arrived slaves. All around them, other gentlemen and ladies from Boston were standing and talking. They were in good humor as they spoke with old friends or chatted cheerfully with new ones. All along the dock a large number of Africans sat alone or huddled together in small groups, waiting to see what would happen to them. It was all a familiar sight in Boston. Massachusetts had been the first of the American colonies to make slavery legal, approving the practice in 1641. Because the harbor allowed excellent access for the ships that carried their valuable human cargo, Boston had become a center of the slave trade in the colonies.

"She's sick, Susanna. Probably won't live very long," John Wheatley replied, as he bent down to examine the sickly child. He knew his wife's soft heart was influencing her thinking and that he would have to be firm. The child, Susanna Wheatley, he was observing did, in fact, have remarkable eyes. They, however, were the only thing about the child that stood out to make her seem a likely purchase. Her tiny arms and legs were sticks covered by loose skin. Her cheeks were hollow, and she was missing her front teeth. Missing teeth was often a symptom of serious diseases such as scurvy or simple malnutrition. Her breathing was labored, suggesting that she had lung disease, possibly even tuberculosis. Even her dark skin seemed to have a yellowing, almost jaundice look. John Wheatley had seen many slaves arrive on the Boston Harbor water front in similar condition, but rarely so young and almost never in such poor shape as the child his wife was watching. More often, slaves as sickly as this child had died during transport, and their bodies had been thrown to the schools of sharks that haunted slave ships. Every slaver was followed by the sharks. They patiently swam in the ships' wakes, waiting to feed on the body of a dead slave thrown overboard or that of a living one who had fallen into depression and jumped. Slaves often chose to die rather than suffer the treatment they received on a slave ship or could no longer endure being taken from their homes and families. This child had been fortunate to escape such an ending. Still, she clearly would not do. As he stood watching his wife, however, John Wheatley feared that nothing he might say would persuade Susanna to change her mind. He was accustomed to his wife's stubbornness, but was, nonetheless, frustrated by it on many occasions. This was such an occasion, for John Wheatley could well see that she would be making an obvious and avoidable mistake if she insisted on buying the sick child.

All around them, John and Susanna Wheatley saw African men and women with a confused but terrified look in their eyes. They were frightened animals caught in a cage waiting for what was sure to be a terrible fate. Although frightened, most were strong and in relatively good health. At least they would recover quickly once given a proper place to live and a few nutritious meals. The women were well suited to the life of a domestic slave, so often referred to in Boston as servants. Had they asked, the Wheatleys would have learned of the child's origins in Senegambia. Women from that region were valued in the American colonies as being good house servants and nannies. The French slaver Joseph Pruneau said of them in his travel journal, "These negroes are very nimble, and hardworking, and have attractive features and are tall."

Other well-dressed men and women from Boston walked among these cowering Africans. Boston was expanding rapidly, and its citizens were becoming prosperous. They had a growing need for slaves and could provide the trade goods the slavers would need when they returned to Africa to again load their ships with stolen Africans. Unlike Susanna Wheatley, these other potential buyers looked carefully before deciding which of these slaves they would purchase. They would stand the Africans and squeeze their arms and legs to test their muscle tone. Potential buyers would have one of the men working on the docks to force them to open their mouths so their teeth could be examined. For the people of Boston, the scene was a normal aspect of life. For the frightened Africans, it was yet another part of a horrifying experience which had begun months before when they had been stolen from their homes. The little girl that had caught Susanna's eye was different in some way. She, too, must have been frightened. But Susanna saw something more than fear in the child's expression. She saw intelligence.

"Maybe," Susanna responded to her husband's reservations. "But there's something about her eyes." Later, Susanna would write of the day she found the girl and describe the "modest demeanor and interesting features of the little stranger."

"I see it, too, but still. . ." John Wheatley's words trailed off. He was convinced that he would be wasting his money to buy the sick little girl. But he knew his wife as well. She was determined that this child would become her companion in her later years. If anyone could nurse the child back to health, it was the strong-willed Susanna Wheatley. John was sure, however, that even her efforts would fail. Not only would he be wasting his money buying the child, his wife would have to endure the despair of watching the little girl die. Susanna had suffered when she had lost two of her own children. He had seen her grief before at the death of a slave, despite the fact that they were, as John Wheatley felt, only property, after all, easily replaced. His wife did not share his thinking about their slaves.

"You need a domestic servant, Susanna," John reminded his wife. "I doubt that even if she lives that child will ever grow into an adult strong enough to be of much use. She will likely be more of a burden than anything else if she does live."

"I don't care, John. I want her." The whole time they had been talking, John saw that his wife's eyes never left the child. Nor did those of the child leave his wife. Now, however, Susanna turned to him, placed her hands firmly on her hips, and stared at her husband with an expression as penetrating as that of the child. John Wheatley had seen the look before. This time, as in the past, he simply shrugged his shoulders and nodded before making one last feeble attempt.

"Susanna…"

"No, John, I want to take a chance on the poor little thing. She's smart, John. I can tell. I'll tend to her, and she'll be fine. You'll see." What John Wheatley did see was that he and his wife, now age fifty-two, had come to the docks seeking a slave to attend to Susanna. What they were leaving with was a child that would require her attention instead.

The child's expression showed that she did not understand what the man and woman were saying. The woman's blonde hair and sparkling eyes captured the child's attention. The man's look was stern, but nothing like the glares and angered expressions she had seen from every other white man she had experienced. What they were saying was not clear. But she knew they were talking about her. And she saw kindness in the woman's expression. She had not seen kindness in many weeks. She had seen disease, hunger, and death. She had seen brutal men and frightened Africans, both men and women. She had seen the men who had abducted her and then those who manned the slave ship treat the women in ways that no child should have experienced. She had grown afraid of everyone whom she encountered. Even the other Africans with whom she had been shipped were strangers to her, with a different language and unfamiliar look about them. Now, however, all she knew to do was to keep looking back at this woman who was obviously interested in her. She could tell this woman was different from any other she had known since being taken from her mother.

Susanna Wheatley and her husband, John, a successful Boston tailor and merchant, had decided to attend the slave sale at which Phyllis, as she would later be called, was offered. Susanna wanted a young, personal servant. The slaves she already owned were older women. She had begun to think of having a young attendant to be her companion during her later years. When she saw the child, she saw in her looks and her demeanor something which she liked. She liked the appearance of the child so much that she chose to ignore all the shortcomings that her husband pointed out. She paid no attention to the severity in his voice as he tried to persuade her to look for another woman in the group that was huddled there on the docks. Because Avery and Gwin, the slavers who were conducting the sale, thought the sickly child would not survive, John Wheatley was able to buy her for what he later called a "trifle." He perhaps paid little more than the four pounds that the slave traders would owe in fees for each slave brought to the docks of Boston. After being bought, the child rode to her new home in Susanna Wheatley's carriage. The black man driving the carriage was unlike any African she had ever seen. He wore well-tailored clothing, much like that worn by the man who sat across from her and next to the woman who had insisted that she go with them. He was clean and groomed. He in no way reminded her of the African men from her village or those who had helped the white men capture her and take her from her home. The city, too, was unlike anything the child had ever seen. Her village had been a small, quiet collection of modest huts and dirt paths. This place was large and filled with tall, wooden and brick buildings. The stone streets bustled with activity. The sounds of commerce filled the air, as did the sweet odors from the shops and kitchens that lined the streets of Boston. All Phyllis had known for weeks was cruelty and fear. Now, her life had changed, dramatically. As she rode from the harbor to the Wheatley home, the little girl began a relationship with Susanna Wheatley which she would later refer to as being like that of family. It was the end of a horrible ordeal that had begun weeks before. It was the beginning of the journey of one of the most remarkable women in American history.

* * *

Like any other six-year-old child from the Senegambia region of West Africa, the little girl welcomed the morning sun. The rainy season had ended in her tropical homeland. The hot and humid days that had followed were perfect for playing outside. The lush jungle that surrounded her village along what is today known as the Gambia River offered many exciting discoveries for a little girl. As she dashed from her family's hut, the girl saw her mother pouring out water to greet the morning sun, which many Africans referred to as Evua. Her family were members of the Fula, or Fulani, tribe. They were Moslems who worshiped Allah as their god. The little girl knew little of these beliefs or of those of other Africans. She knew only that her mother practiced this ritual each morning. It was the only thing about her life in Africa that she would be able to recall in her later years. It was the only thing she would be able to tell her captors.

The little girl was stolen from her home sometime in the spring of 1761. Her abduction may have resulted from a raid on her village. Such raids were common throughout West Africa in the eighteenth century. Many African tribal kings captured slaves to trade to Europeans or to serve their own needs. During such raids, villages were set on fire and the people were kidnapped as they fled into the jungle or killed if they tried to resist capture. Or she may have been stolen by a small group of men who would hide near such villages and snatch children who had wandered away from the safety of their homes and parents to sell as slaves. But like all Africans captured in the back country of Senegambia, she was marched to the coast in a coffle, a line of slaves tied together. The journey was often long and brutal. Many who had been captured would die, even during these first days of their captivity. While traveling in the coffle, they would receive little food, and it would be of poor quality. The days were long, with little rest. The nights were worse, for in the dark the abducted Africans' worst thoughts about what would happen to them seemed all the more likely to occur. The enslaved Africans were often mistreated by their captors who wanted to make clear the punishment that would result from any efforts to resist their enslavement. Once the coffle had arrived at the coast, the child was confined in a barracoon along with other slaves. There she waited to be sold and taken from her home once and for all. The European slave traders offered glass beads, guns, and whiskey to the African leaders who were involved with the slave trade. Children like the little girl were not prized as much as strong men or healthy young women. However, once taken they were easy to handle and would bring enough of a price to load them onto a slave ship bound for the West.

The barracoon in which the little girl was forced to live was probably on the island of Goree, just off the coast of West Africa. It was little more than a wooden stockade in which the slaves would be divided into groups and herded together into small booths and prepared for shipment. Separated in this fashion, they were easier to handle once untied and less likely to spread disease. If she had been abducted alone rather than taken in a raid on her village, she might have recognized no one with whom she was now imprisoned.

Life in a barracoon was difficult to survive. The captured Africans were offered no sanitation. Many developed worms from the poor food they were given or suffered from other diseases. When they grew so sick that were obviously no longer property of any value, they were killed. Their bodies were either burned or thrown outside the walls where the hyenas would feed on the discarded corpses. The indignities which they suffered in death did, at least, put an end to what they had endured while alive.

* * *

"Hush now, child. They don't hurt you too much."

The words were not familiar to the little girl. The tone in the woman's voice, however, was reassuring. Still, as she looked through the tears that clouded her eyes, the little girl could see that the woman who spoke them was grimacing and staring ahead at the men who were branding the slaves in the barracoon.

"They only burn the women a little—"

A man's shriek interrupted. The little girl and her companion were now close enough to smell the burning of flesh. The little girl's stomach lurched as the smell sickened her. She feared that she would become visibly sick but managed to hide her reaction to the scene she had just witnessed.

"Don't want to mark them so the men don't want them." The woman continued to talk, though the child did not understand her words. The quiet tones did, however, help calm the child a bit as she waited to be marked with the sign of the man who now owned her.

By the time she was next in the line, the little girl had braced herself. She knew the branding would hurt, but at least it was about to be over.

"Careful with that one," a rough voice from one of the men doing the branding cut the air. "She'll make a fine prize for her master when she's a bit older. Don't want to leave a bad scar."

These words, as well, meant nothing to the little girl, but the cruelty in them and in the laughter that followed was something she had known since being taken from her home. And as the hot iron pressed into the flesh of her chest she stood firm until the odor of her own burning skin filled her nose and she again felt ill. When the man pulled the hot iron back from her chest, she looked down at the redness which would give her a permanent mark. She did not know that the mark pressed into her flesh signaled her final loss of freedom. She understood only that she had been hurt and that she knew no reason to explain the cruelty to which she was being subjected.

"Move along," the voice said again, and a rough hand pushed the little girl aside. She tried to not be sick for fear that she might be considered what she had heard the men call a Mackron, a defective piece of property to be killed in order that she not be further trouble or spread the disease that had made her sick.

"You did good child," the woman who had spoken to her earlier whispered. The child may not have known the words the woman spoke, but she sensed that they were kind. Still, she had no smile to offer in thanks.

Back in her booth, she huddled in a corner and watched the movements of the other men and women who surrounded her through a fog of tears.

* * *

When she finally left Senegambia in the spring or summer of 1761, it was aboard the slaving ship, the Phyllis. The ship was captained by Peter Gwin. It was making the second leg of the Middle Passage. She would later take the name of the ship as her given name and be known as Phyllis.

The Middle Passage was as brutal for captured slaves as it was financially beneficial to European trading companies. Some slavers practiced what was known as loose packing and shipped slaves under conditions that were tolerable, if inhumane. Other slave ship captains believed it better to tight pack their human cargo. More slaves died during transport as a result of the crowded and dirty conditions. The thinking of such slave traders was that although more of the Africans died, they still arrived in the West Indies or North America with a larger cargo to sell. Phyllis probably experienced a loose pack. Men and women were separated for the journey. Phyllis was confined with seventy to eighty other young women. All were packed into a space in the ship's hold that was thirteen feet wide, twenty-five feet long, and less than six feet high. At least with a loose pack, the slaves were able to sit or stand upright and not forced to spend the passage lying on their backs in coffin-like compartments. There Phyllis sat during the long weeks of the trip, not understanding what was happening to her, and certainly not knowing why she was being treated with such brutality. She knew only that she had been taken from her home and family.

Surviving the Middle Passage was difficult for any slave. It would have been particularly difficult for a child as young as Phyllis. She would have had two meals each day, one around 8:00 a.m. and the second around 4:00 p.m. These meals occasionally included a bit of beef or pork. They were more likely to have been composed of boiled yams, rice, or the pulp from boiled horse beans brought from Europe. Poor food was not the only concern the child would have faced. She would have experienced or observed other forms of mistreatment. Most slave ship captains allowed members of their crew to mistreat the women slaves. There is no record of the type of captain Peter Gwin was. Perhaps he was one of those who during clear weather and calm seas allowed slaves to leave the ship's hold and dance on its deck for exercise. There they could escape for a time the excessive heat created by so many bodies packed closely together. On deck, their noses were free of the smell of vinegar which was used to disinfect the hold of the ship. When Phyllis arrived in Boston, Massachusetts on July 11, 1761, however, she was frail and sickly. She was probably suffering from flux, a disease of the digestive system that resulted from poor food and unsanitary living conditions that left her weak. Her breathing was heavy, a sure sign of some type of lung disease. She was also missing her two front teeth. In such pitiful condition, Phyllis was moved once again into a filthy warehouse, not unlike the barracoon in which she had lived except that it was covered by a roof. There she was held until an auction could be arranged to sell her and the other Africans who had survived the journey. So few slaves arrived on the slave ship, the Phyllis; and many of them, like Phyllis, were in such poor health that the ship's owner, Timothy Fitch, scolded his captain.

The auction at which Phyllis was sold was announced in the August 3, 1761, edition of the *Boston Evening Post*:

To Be Sold

A parcel of likely Negroes, imported from Africa, cheap for cash, or short Credit, Enquire of John Avery, at his House next Door to the White-Horse, or at the a Store adjoining to said Avery's Distill-House, at the South End, near the South Market.

Avery was an experienced Boston businessman. He would have agreed with Captain Gwin that the child, Phyllis, was likely going to die and hardly worth putting up for sale. She was what slavers called a "refuse Negro." Nonetheless, covered with only a dirty piece of carpet which offered little protection from the weather, Phyllis was offered for sale and captured the eye of Susanna Wheatley.

Chapter II

Reading, Writing, and Religion

"Hurry, Mother!" exclaimed Mary Wheatley. The two women walked quickly through their large house at the corner of King Street and Market Lane in Boston. "You must see what Phyllis has done!"

Mary Wheatley and her twin brother Nathaniel were eighteen when Phyllis became part of their household and was given the family name as her own. Although twins, they did not look alike. Mary had the light coloring and delicate features of her mother. Nathaniel was tall and rugged. He was not, however, a stern man, as John Wheatley so often proved to be. Both Mary and Nathaniel had been as kind to the little girl as their mother. They had also seen immediately, as Susanna had, that there was something special about the child. As Mary and Susanna entered the parlor at the front of the house, they saw Phyllis holding a piece of chard wood from the fire that had burned the night before. She was using it to mark on the walls of the room. She was so occupied with her marking that she did not notice that Susanna and Mary had entered the room. Nor had she noticed the look first of surprise and then gentle laughter which Susanna could not suppress.

"Phyllis," Susanna Wheatley said quietly.

The little girl responded immediately. She looked down and tried to hide the charcoal she held in her hand. Phyllis, however, had never been able to pretend with Susanna Wheatley. When she realized that she could not hide the piece of charred wood, she moved as if about to flee the room before realizing that running would serve no purpose. She was caught. That was all there was to it.

"No, Phyllis, it's all right," Susanna said again as she saw the child's frighten reaction.

"Mother," added Mary, "she wants to write. Look at her marks. They're not right, but she's trying to make letters."

Susanna looked a moment at the smudges on the wall and then back at Phyllis. Phyllis continued to sit quietly in the floor. She had not said a word since being discovered doing something she feared would cause her to be punished. Phyllis had not received such treatment since coming to live in the Wheatley home. She had, however, seen other slaves punished for their bad behavior.

"Is that right, Phyllis? Are you trying to write the way Mary and Nathaniel do?" Susanna Wheatley asked as she bent to look Phyllis directly in the eyes.

"Yes," the little girl whispered and nodded her head. She had quickly learned to speak English after becoming part of the Wheatley household. Also, she had often watched as the Nathaniel and Mary Wheatley did their school work. Phyllis had been fascinated when she learned that the marks they were making and those which appeared in their books had meanings that Mary and Nathaniel understood. She marveled as well at the fact that both the Wheatley children seemed to so much enjoy learning the meaning of the marks.

Susanna Wheatley stood and looked at her daughter. Then she studied the marks on the wall and the child who had made them. After a few moments, she had made up her mind what she needed to do.

"Then Mary will teach you. And to read, as well."

Mary Wheatley smiled to indicate that she would welcome the task of teaching this special child to read and write. Phyllis returned the warm smile. From the day she had met Susanna Wheatley on the docks at Boston Harbor, Phyllis had realized that her mistress was a kind woman. Now, she had yet another example of that kindness. Had the Wheatleys lived in one of the Southern colonies, Susanna would have been breaking the law by teaching a slave to read. In the South, slave owners who used their bought Africans primarily for labor on their plantations were afraid that if slaves were able to read and write, they would learn ways to seek their freedom. Reading might expose them to

Abolitionist ideas which were beginning to take hold in the Northern colonies. There slavery did not serve the major economic purpose that it did in the South. Slave owners in the North used their human property more as servants than laborers. Phyllis, of course, did not know such things; nor was Susanna Wheatley at all concerned that by teaching Phyllis to read she would be risking the child's becoming dissatisfied with her life as a slave. Susanna only knew that the child wanted to learn to read and write and that Mary was willing to teach her. Phyllis simply knew that she was going to learn to read and write!

* * *

From the moment she had become part of the Wheatley household, Phyllis had been treated more as a member of the family than a slave. John Wheatley had been right when he had warned his wife about the sickly child's prospects. Phyllis had struggled to survive, even with the excellent care she received from Susanna. She had, moreover, never grown strong and suffered periodically from various afflictions, mostly with allergies and breathing difficulties. The domestic chores she was given were, therefore, simple to perform, usually minor dusting. Most of her day was spent as a companion to Susanna Wheatley and her children. Phyllis was not allowed to associate directly with the other slaves the Wheatleys owned. She even ate at the family table. It was the practice of many slaves, especially after being freed, to take the names of their masters. For Phyllis, taking the name of Wheatley was even more appropriate. She was in many ways protected by Susanna as if she were a member of the family.

* * *

"John," Susanna Wheatley said as she entered her husband's study. "Phyllis is visiting with the Harringtons."

"Yes," John Wheatley said, looking up from the stack of papers that cluttered his desk. "I recall she had been invited."

"The weather is looking as if it will storm."

John Wheatley nodded. He saw the fearful look in his wife's eyes. It suddenly occurred to him what was causing her anxiety.

"We mustn't let Phyllis walk home in the rain," he said.

"She'll be sick if she does," Susanna said with an almost frantic sense of urgency.

John Wheatley stood and started out of the room. "I'll send Prince to get her."

"Mrs. Harrington might send her with one of their servants."

"Perhaps," John answered, "but she may not be aware of how serious Phyllis' health problems are. I best send Prince."

"Thank you," Susanna offered as she approached her husband and kissed him on the cheek. In that moment, she recalled how much her husband had wanted her not to select Phyllis from the slaves on the docks. Still, he had granted her wish that day and never questioned the treatment she offered Phyllis. Susanna knew her husband. He saw the Africans they owned as property and did not develop attachments to them. But he loved his wife and allowed her to treat Phyllis with whatever kindness she thought appropriate.

Prince hurried to the Harringtons' house when John Wheately had told him to go for Phyllis. Like the other slaves the Wheatleys owned, he was aware of the special place Phyllis had in the mistress' heart. Many of the others, especially those who attended to the house, resented Phyllis. She was expected to do far less than the others. They felt that because Phyllis did so little that they were expected to do more than was fair. Prince, however, had not forgotten the terrified little girl he first saw the day John and Susanna Wheatley had escorted Phyllis from the harbor docks a few years earlier. Seeing her that day, Prince understood that Phyllis would never be a very suitable piece of property for the Wheatleys, but had for whatever reason been selected by the mistress. He understood as well when sent to pick her up at the Harringtons' house he better do all he could to return with her before the dark clouds that were gathering over Boston let loose the rain that they carried.

When he arrived at the Harrington home, Prince breathed a sigh of relief. Phyllis was standing on the front porch of the impressive, three story frame house. There, she and Mrs. Harrington seemed to be studying the weather. When Phyllis saw Prince bring the carriage to a stop along the street, however, she quickly took leave of her hostess. She hurried to the carriage where Prince was waiting to offer her a hand into the passenger compartment.

"I want to ride with you," Phyllis said.

"With me?"

"Yes, I've never ridden up high. I want to sit next to you."

Prince was uncertain. He knew that Phyllis was to be treated as a member of the family. It would not be appropriate for her to ride next to a slave, despite the fact that she was a slave herself. He was also aware of Phyllis' health problems and that she would be better protected riding inside the carriage. On the other hand, if she "was" a member of the family, then he was obligated to honor her request.

"You best stay out of the air," Prince offered feebly.

"The air is good for me," Phyllis answered.

"But we goin' have rain any time now."

"You'll have us home before the rain begins, won't you?"

"I 'spect so," Prince said. "But I cain't be sure. You best ride inside."

"No. You help me up. I want to sit next to you." Prince nodded his head, but offered no smile as he gave Phyllis his hand and she climbed to the driver's seat of the carriage.

John, Susanna and Mary Wheatley were all waiting on the steps to their home when Prince drove up, with Phyllis sitting at his side. The wind had become severe and the storm would break at any moment, leaving Susanna in a panic about Phyllis. Prince saw them and felt a knot form immediately in his stomach.

"That saucy varlet," Susanna Wheatley muttered when she saw Phyllis sitting next to Prince. "What can he be thinking."

"She's all right, now," John Wheatley offered.

"I don't care," Susanna said. "Prince had no business putting her at risk. I want him punished, John."

"Susanna…"

"I want him punished." The look his wife gave let John Wheatley know that she was in no mood to argue.

As quickly as the carriage stopped, Prince locked the brakes and jumped down to help Phyllis. She took his hand gently and smiled her thanks. He glared back, knowing that he was likely to be punished if the look in the mistress' eyes was any indication.

"What do you mean, letting her sit beside you, Prince!" Susanna Wheatley chastised. Prince offered no response.

"I wanted…." Phyllis began.

"You go with Mary. Get out of this wind. Prince, you tend that horse and then you find Mr. Wheatley."

"But…," Phyllis tried again.

"Go on, Prince."

"Yes'm."

Susanna Wheatley hurried back to the house as Mary took Phyllis by the hand. Mary pinched her mouth as if to say to Phyllis there was nothing to do. Her mother was angry. Neither said anything, however. As she looked back at a dejected Prince, Phyllis began to see just how different her place really was compared with that of the other slaves. The decision to sit by Prince was her own. Now he was going to be punished because of her action. It was one of those times when Phyllis was reminded that despite the Wheatleys' kindness toward her, they were still slave owners. Though they might treat her as something different, the other Africans were their property. And they treated their other slaves as just that, as property.

* * *

Phyllis Wheatley proved herself to be not just an enthusiastic student, but a gifted one as well. In less than two years after being discovered making crude marks on the wall with a piece of chard wood, she was reading and writing. Even more impressive was the fact that she was reading from English and classical literature, even works on geography, astronomy, and history. Most important, Phyllis learned to read the Bible. She committed herself to her study with a passion that everyone in the Wheatley household admired. She demonstrated this passion for learning when she discovered that the students at Harvard had created a fuss because of being served butter that had grown stale. Phyllis felt these young men did not appreciate the wonderful opportunity to study they had been given. She conveyed her thoughts in her poem "To the University of Cambridge, in New England":

Students, to you 't is given to scan the heights
Above, to traverse the etherial space,
And mark the systems of revolving worlds.
Still more, ye sons of science, ye receive
The blissful news by messengers from heaven,
How Jesus' blood for your redemption flows.
See him, with hands outstretched upon the cross!

Phyllis' desire to write poetry was clearly the product of her reading. The form of her poetry, especially the use of the rhyming couplet, shows the influence of the English poets she read. She also wrote poems about special occasions. Such verses, appropriately called occasional poems, were popular in England. The poet she most enjoyed reading and whose works she imitated was Alexander Pope.

* * *

"You seem especially occupied with your reading tonight," Nathaniel Wheatley observed. He had been watching Phyllis for several minutes as the two of them sat in the parlor of the Wheatley home. He had seldom seen such a look of concentration on her face. And yet, the entire time he had been watching, Phyllis had not turned a page. She was not reading. She was thinking. "Another piece by Mr. Pope?"

Nathaniel's words called Phyllis from her thoughts and she nodded. "'An Essay on Man.'"

"I see," Nathaniel nodded. "One of my favorite poems by Mr. Pope as well."

Phyllis remained quiet, but was well aware of Nathaniel's staring at her, trying to look behind her eyes and discover her thoughts.

"You've found a passage that either confuses you or troubles you, Phyllis."

Phyllis nodded. "He says, 'What would this man? Now upward will he soar,/And little less than angel, would be more.'"

Nathaniel did not speak. He waited, astonished by this young woman's depth of thought. He remembered the trembling, frail creature that his parents had brought home a few years earlier. Even now, she was little more than a girl. Yet, she was not simply reading Alexander Pope, but also feeling the weight of his words. He had studied this particular work at length and struggled with its ideas about the place of man in God's universe.

"What is it about that passage that you find so provoking?"

Phyllis drew up her eyebrows and scrunched her mouth. Her breathing was strained, but tonight not from illness, but rather concentration as she tried to form her thoughts into words.

"He is questioning why man has to try to be that which God did not make him to be."

"I agree," Nathaniel said.

"But it is more than that. He suggests in other passages that it is sin if we try to be more than God intended."

"I agree with that as well. Why does that trouble you?"

"Then I am sinning," Phyllis said suddenly, "by reading and writing."

Nathaniel's eyes popped. Her words had a crushing weight. He had not anticipated the path their discussion would take. "Why is that a sin for you?"

"Because. I am a slave. My place is to serve my mistress. Not to learn to read or write."

Nathaniel had long been aware of Phyllis' gifts, but never had he seen the depth of her thought as he was seeing in that moment. And he had met few people who could think so intelligently about how what they read applied to their own lives. He had known teachers and scholars. For them, however, the ideas they read were just that, ideas. For Phyllis, they were more. They were propositions which she felt compelled to consider within the context of her own actions.

"But your mistress wants you to read and to write," Nathaniel said after a few moments.

"Then, does she not sin as well, by letting me do something beyond my place?"

"Why," Nathaniel asked slowly, "is it not your place to read and to write?"

"Because I am a slave. God made me a slave."

"God didn't make you a slave, Phyllis. Men did."

Phyllis considered Nathaniel's words a few moments before speaking. Had she been talking with anyone else, she knew she would have felt the need to speak less openly. Nathaniel, however, had always seemed interested in her thoughts. She wanted to accept his resolution to her dilemma. His response, however, was not sufficient.

"Then by keeping me a slave, is that a sin? If it wasn't God's plan? And isn't everything that happens God's plan?"

"You mean," Nathaniel asked, "that if you are a slave, then God intended you to be? No matter how that came to happen?"

"Yes, or that if He didn't, it is sin to make me a slave. To do so is to force me from that place where I belong in God's plan."

Nathaniel sat back in his chair. He had no answer. Phyllis' thoughts were clearly those of an Abolitionist. And yet, she was not presenting them in that way. Her questions were theological, not political. All she was trying to do was understand God. And Alexander Pope's words had given her no answers. Rather, what he wrote, combined with her position in life as property, left her confused. Yet, in her confusion, she was showing a profound understanding of two of the most challenging social and theological questions of the eighteenth century, that of the nature of God and his creation, as well as that of slavery.

"Somehow," Nathaniel said after a while, "I don't think Mr. Pope took into account the way his words might sound to someone living as a slave."

Phyllis chewed on Nathaniel's response. "But, if what he says is correct, it should be as true for me as for anyone."

"Yes . . . it should."

"Then where do I look for an answer?" Phyllis asked.

Nathaniel laughed. "I fear that asking me has been of little help."

Phyllis smiled. She had not meant to suggest that she found Nathaniel's thoughts meaningless. "I didn't mean...."

"Oh, I know. I wasn't thinking you were being critical of me. It just struck me. I studied Mr. Pope. And I thought... I think I understand him. I simply never looked beyond his poem to examine life. That is what you do, Phyllis."

"What I do?"

"You don't just read to understand the words. You think about what they mean, for you. For all of us," Nathaniel said.

"Perhaps I should not question."

Nathaniel smiled. "I don't think you have a choice, Phyllis. You will always be asking questions. It is who you are. You will never be satisfied with simple answers to big questions."

Phyllis had not found a sufficient answer to her question. She had, however, found in Nathaniel's words reassurance that she was not doing anything wrong by asking it.

* * *

Susanna Wheatley enthusiastically encouraged Phyllis and her efforts to write poetry. When Phyllis told her that she often would lie awake at night and compose lines in her head, but then could not remember them the next day, Susanna responded quickly. Not only was Phyllis provided writing materials to keep by her bed, she also had candles and a fire to give her the necessary light and warmth to work. And work she did. In her short lifetime, she produced an estimated 145 poems and numerous letters.

Phyllis' reading of the Bible, and the influence of the Wheatleys' strong religious beliefs, also brought her to Christianity. In 1770, at age 16, Phyllis Wheatley joined the Old South Church. She had been attending services at least twice a week. She sat in the section of the church which was referred to as either the "African Corner" or "Nigger Heaven." In 1771, she was baptized by the famous minister, the Reverend Dr. Samuel Cooper. Very few Africans brought to America were baptized at this time. When the slave trade in Europe and the colonies had first begun, however, the Catholic Church had approved of slavery only if the slaves were baptized before being shipped from Africa. To accommodate this demand, slavers had employed priests to conduct mass baptisims of captured Africans before loading them onto their ships. That practice had ended by the time Phyllis had been taken captive, particularly for American slavers because the colonials had little regard for the demands of the Catholic Church. However, the influence of the Wheatleys and their dedication to Phyllis made her special. Even outside their home she was usually not treated as a typical slave. Often, when joining the Wheatleys and visiting in the home of one of Boston's prosperous families, Phyllis would be offered a place at the family table. Though she joined the Wheatleys at their table, on such occasions she usually asked to be excused and to eat at a side table. One exception to this practice occurred when Phyllis was visiting in the home of Colonel and Mrs. Fitch, the owner of the slaving ship that had brought Phyllis to Boston. She accepted an invitation to join the family for tea, but was then confronted with the objections of the Fitch children. Rather than ask to be excused, Phyllis began telling the family some of the stories she knew. She made such an impression that even the children changed their minds about having a slave share their meal.

In almost every respect, Phyllis Wheatley was an extraordinary child. She certainly was not a typical slave. She was unique even in New England society where slaves were seen somewhat differently than they were in the Southern colonies. Though treated as a member of the family, she was, nonetheless, not free. And this fact makes her becoming only the second woman in America to publish poetry even more amazing.

Chapter III

Literary Success

In 1767, when Phyllis Wheatley was sixteen, her first published work, "On Messrs. Hussey and Coffin," appeared in the *Newport Mercury.* Hussey and Coffin had been guests in the Wheatley home. There, they told of their narrow escape when their ship had sunk during a storm off Cape Cod. It was the perfect subject for Phyllis to try her hand at writing an occasional poem. The poem is not especially notable; the accomplishment of its being published is. That a slave had learned to read and write well enough to write poetry, much less to have that poetry published, was not what New England society would have expected. Moreover, Phyllis became only the second woman to publish poetry in America. The first was Ann Bradstreet. Three years later, Phyllis would publish the poem that brought her to the attention of the people in society who would help her career as a writer.

In 1770, the noted minister George Whitefield preached a series of sermons at the Old South Church in Boston which the Wheatleys attended. Whitefield was participating in a movement in America referred to as the Great Awakening. Like many other preachers, Whitefield believed that the American colonists had become overly concerned with political matters instead of religion. The purpose of the Great Awakening and the objective of the ministers who led it was to reestablish in the colonies a zeal for religion which had seemed to fade as political issues became increasingly important. Phyllis attended the sermons of Whitefield. She possibly even met him as a guest in the Wheatley home. In addition to Whitefield's powerful preaching style,

Phyllis would have been impressed by his effort to preach to Negroes attending his sermons. Although he himself felt that slavery was justified by the Bible, part of Whitefield's message was that Jesus was an "impartial saviour" for whom skin color did not matter. A month after this appearance in Boston, however, Whitefield died suddenly. The impact he had on Phyllis and his sudden death encouraged the young poet to write and publish her first major work, "On the Death of the Rev'd Mr. George Whitefield—1770." In this poem, Phyllis directed the following lines at Whitefield's patron, Selina Hastings, the Countess of Huntingdon:

Great Countess, we Americans revere
Thy name, and mingle in thy grief sincere;
New England deeply feels, the orphans mourn,
Their more than father will no more return.

With the assistance of Susanna Wheatley, who had supported Whitefield's work in America and who corresponded with the Countess of Huntingdon, such lines brought Phyllis Wheatley to the attention of her future patron. When the poem was published as a broadside in Boston and London in 1771, Phyllis Wheatley's literary career was underway.

With the success of Phyllis' first printed poems, Susanna Wheatley began to think of publishing a book of her talented slave's work. In 1772, she and Phyllis issued an advertisement for potential buyers in the February, March, and April issues of the Boston Censor. Such efforts to enlist support were necessary for an unknown poet. Printers were reluctant to go to the expense of producing books which they were not sure would sell. A book by a slave, despite her success with two published works, was certainly a project with no guarantee of making money. These ads, however, proved unsuccessful. Susanna and Phyllis began to understand that not enough readers in America were interested in the writing of a slave for a published book of her poems to be successful.

Susanna Wheatley was not defeated by this failure, however. If Phyllis' poems could not attract American readers, they might be successful in England. She told the captain of her husband's ship, Robert Calef, to seek a printer in London who would publish Phyllis' poems. Calef did so. Archibald Bell, a minor publisher of religious material and fierce opponent of slavery, agreed to print Phyllis' book. Bell's decision was certainly encouraged by the fact that the Countess of Huntingdon supported the publication and agreed to have the volume dedicated to her. He did, however, feel that his audience would demand some proof that the poems had in fact been written by an African and a slave.

* * *

For years, the Old Colony House had served as Boston's Town Hall. Issues of great importance to the colony had been debated within its halls. The finest minds and most politically distinguished men of Massachusetts had walked the corridors of the building. There they had discussed ideas which were unknown to most of the people of the colony and generally directed the course of government of not only Boston, but of Massachusetts and the other colonies as well. On this early autumn day in 1772, a black woman of no importance accompanied by the son of her master, Nathaniel Wheatley, approached the Old Colony House to resolve a different issue under question. Phyllis Wheatley had visited with many of Boston's most distinguished families. She had experienced the religious zeal of the pastors who had opened the colonies to the Great Awakening. She had read the words of the finest thinkers of the Enlightenment and discussed those ideas within the comfort of her own home with Nathaniel Wheatley. Nonetheless, carrying a manuscript of poems that she had written over the past two years, she approached the building with both dread and uncertainty.

The grounds of the Old Colony House held a particular beauty in the autumn. Large oak and maple tress were painted with the reds and golds that made New England such a beautiful environment in the fall.

It was nothing like Phyllis' original home, with its lush green that never changed. Although she had only vague memories of Senagambia, Phyllis was aware of the contrast. She was aware, as well, of the difference between her station in life and that of the men she was going to meet.

"I don't belong here," Phyllis said to Nathaniel as she stopped to look at the Old Colony House. Standing there, she studied its ornate molding and delicate glass panes that graced the windows. It stood perfectly situated, surrounded by other buildings and homes that spoke of the greatness of Boston. Phyllis understood that she had come for a second time in her life to a foreign place.

Nathaniel took her hand tenderly. Susanna Wheatley had asked him to accompany Phyllis for many reasons. The most important of these was that he had been the first to grasp the depth of thought Phyllis possessed. After his discussion with her about Alexander Pope's "Essay on Man," Nathaniel had realized that his mother's personal servant was more than a prodigy. Her gifts ran deep. Her ability to wrestle with complex ideas was beyond that of most men, educated men, white men.

"What do you know of the men who will question me?"

"They are just men, Phyllis," Nathaniel said quietly. "Regardless of the positions they hold. They may be your social superiors. But you can think and reason as well as they can."

Phyllis turned a questioning eye on Nathaniel. "What will they ask me?" Nathaniel shrugged. There was no way to know. He did know, however, that the frail, timid woman he was escorting would be able to handle herself well, regardless of the topics she might be asked to discuss.

From the moment that Susanna Wheatley had decided that Phyllis should publish her poetry, this day had been inevitable. For her to place a poem or two in a newspaper was one thing. To ask potential subscribers to her book to commit in advance to buy it, another. Phyllis would have to be able to prove that she, a female slave, was the true author of the poems. In fact, the primary attraction of her work was that it had been written by a slave. In many ways, the quality of the poems did not matter. Readers would buy the book to serve their curiosity. They would want to see what abilities this unusual African had. Her book would add much to the debate which was taking place in Europe and the colonies about the intellectual ability of Negroes. A fundamental rationale used to support the institution of slavery was that the black Africans were inferior to whites.

To prove that she was the author of the poems she presumed to publish, Phyllis was to be tested by eighteen of Massachusetts' most learned men. Their questions would determine whether she had the mental faculties and scholarly capacity to have written the poems she now carried with her. Whether out of loyalty to John Wheatley or curiosity to see this slave said to have such skill, they had agreed to assemble and test Phyllis. They had agreed, as well, to sign a document testifying to their decision about her authorship. The only one among them who had met Phyllis before was Thomas Woolbridge, a representative of the Earl of Dartmouth who would be instrumental in seeing Phyllis' work published in London. His, however, was the only mind made up in the matter.

"Let's go, Phyllis," Nathaniel said quietly. Together they entered the Old Colony House and Phyllis was then led into a room filled with her panel of judges. There they stood, talking in small groups, huddled around the large fireplace where dancing yellow flames cut the slight chill in the air. They were indeed a distinguished group, dressed in waistcoats and tight fitting breeches that stretched to their knees. Some wore powdered white wigs. Others dressed more simply, with their own hair pulled tight to the back or cut short. What they shared, however, was a look of severity. One man in particular seemed to be trying to stare a hole in Phyllis. She would later learn that his name was Reverend Charles Chauncy. He was not a large man, but was, nonetheless, imposing. Chauncy knew that the Wheatleys had been instrumental in hosting the pastors of the Great Awakening and promoting their activities. Chauncy disapproved of the Great Awakening, for it had encouraged woman and even blacks to participate in religious services in ways that he felt inappropriate. Phyllis would have been to him the embodiment of that which he rejected. His stern look, right in her direction, left Phyllis certain that she was making a mistake appearing before this group. He made her feel that she was misguided to even try to publish poetry, perhaps even to write it. It was, however, her mistress' orders that she subject herself even to a man like Chauncy, so Phyllis stood her ground as the men were introduced to her: Thomas Huthcinson, Governor of Massachusetts; Andrew Oliver, Lieutenant Governor of Massachu-setts; the Reverend Samuel Cooper; James Bowdoin, a leading scholar and proponent of the ideals of the Enlightenment; the pragmatic John Hancock, who opposed that which Bowdoin represented and saw his thinking too much influenced by the European mind; the Reverend Samuel Mather, son of the famous clergyman Cotton Mather. The names went on, and Phyllis did not recognize them all. Those she had heard before, however, were such as to make her certain that she should leave. She barely heard the preliminaries addressed to the group by Governor Hutchinson, but then a voice rang clearly.

"I've seen hundreds of slaves," said Thomas Hubbard, a man who had in been a slave trader in the past. "I've never seen one with the abilities that you are said to have." Phyllis stared at the man. He had not asked her a question. No matter how remarkable she might be considered or how well-treated in the Wheatley home, Phyllis knew her place. She waited for the question. Hubbard stared at her, confused.

"Ask her a question Thomas, for heaven's sake," said the man introduced as John Hancock. Phyllis wanted to smile. She appreciated the words and the look of the man who had interjected himself. Hubbard, on the other hand, scowled.

"Very well. Who was Apollo? One of the poems you are said to have written alludes to him."

"Apollo was the sun god in Greek mythology," Phyllis said with no emotion. "The sun, as we see it, is the wake of his chariot as he rides through the sky."

"And you believe this?" Hubbard said abruptly.

"No sir, it is an image in Greek mythology. God made the sun. As he made all that is."

"And you understand God, then do you?" asked Reverend Chauncy. This new voice surprised Phyllis, and she turned abruptly to face the glaring eyes of the man who had spoken.

"I understand what the Bible says of God. God is to us, as He was to Job, in many ways a mystery. So I cannot say that I understand God."

"Well said," Phyllis heard from her one sure advocate, Thomas Woolbridge.

Chauncey, on the other hand, was not impressed. "Is that the way you were taught by Reverend Whitefield?" The man's knowledge of her startled Phyllis. She had heard and learned much about Christianity from Whitefield. She had, moreover, published a poem in which she referred to Whitefield as a saint and spoke of his desire "to see America excel."

"It is what I have learned from my own reading of the Bible, sir. But many ministers of God's word have helped me understand that which I have read."

"And your reading in the Bible has led you to see God as a mystery?" asked Governor Hutchinson.

"Yes sir."

"Perhaps," Chauncey observed as an opening in the conversation developed, "God is a mystery to you because you are not capable of understanding Him." Phyllis stood mute. The others in the room were quiet as well. The lapse was uncomfortable for Phyllis, and she stepped from foot to foot, not realizing her actions.

"If you have read the philosophical works you are said to have read, you would be familiar with Mr. Hume's writings." The statement came from James Bowdoin.

"Yes sir." Bowdoin had not asked a question, but Phyllis understood his meaning.

"You are aware, then, that he has argued with, I think, great insight that Negroes are fundamentally inferior to whites. That they are not able to deal with complex ideas and must live their lives in comfortable servitude."

"Yes sir," Phyllis said. This time she waited for the question. She knew that this was how such men debated. They would make observations which they felt sure would bait a response from their opponents. She was there to establish her intellectual abilities. She was not there to present herself as their equal. She was a slave. She would wait for the question.

"And," Bowdoin continued. "Do you agree?"

"Mr. Hubbard," Phyllis said quietly, "indicated that he had never seen one of my race with the abilities I am said to have. With respect to him, to you all, these are not abilities which one can see. I have little contact with other slaves. I have talked with some, however, whom I believe to be as intelligent as anyone I know." The moment she spoke, Phyllis feared that her words might well offend the men questioning her. But there was nothing to be done. The words were spoken, and they conveyed what she believes. "I have had opportunity. They have not." The room grew quiet as Phyllis spoke. Her words began to build and with them her confidence. "Mr. Hume, I suppose, has only observed Negroes who have been enslaved. And not slaves like myself. They have lived lives without opportunity. How can he judge what they might be capable of if this is so?"

"Then," Governor Hutchinson began, "you do see yourself as being unique."

"I see myself, sir, as one who has been given unique opportunity."

"Yes. Very well said," a quiet voice sounded.

Phyllis looked again at Mr. Woolbridge. This time, however, her support had come from the man introduced as Mr. Hancock.

"Well, John," said Bowdoin, "we all know that your thinking is a bit different. You despise the blessings of European thought."

"I despise, sir," offered Hancock, "the taint of irrational superiority. The Europeans in general and the British in particular, use such inflated images of themselves to justify holding the colonies in servitude. Mr. Hume is one of the worst of this sort of arrogant brood."

"And what of young Mr. Jefferson? He is a philosopher of the European mind." Bowdoin said.

"Yes," responded Hancock, "and he also thinks Negroes inferior, as did your David Hume. And he owns slaves. And..."

"And . . .?"

"And he is wrong!" Hancock shouted as he turned from the group.

As the two men debated, Phyllis stood patiently. She wanted to leave. Her breathing was growing heavy, and she had begun to grow faint.

"You enjoy the writings of Mr. Pope, I am told," said Reverend Mather Byles of the Hollis Street Congregational Church. His was a statement as well. It was made with such ease, however, that Phyllis responded by nodding.

"I have had some correspondence with Mr. Pope," Byles said. Phyllis smiled. "Are you familiar with his discussion of natural order?"

"I have read his writings on that subject."

"'Where, one step broken, the great scale's destroy'd:/From Nature's chain whatever link you strike,/Tenth, or ten thousandth,'" Byles began quoting.

"...breaks the chain alike," Phyllis completed the passage. She was startled at her impertinence. The room was startled at her knowledge.

"Impressive, Miss Wheatley," Byles replied. Throughout the room, the men who had gathered to observe and judge Phyllis watched the exchange that was developing between the one of their number who was most familiar with the poet whom Phyllis Wheatley particularly admired and whose work she imitated. Phyllis, on the other hand, was left mute. She had never before been addressed formally. Reverend Byles had surprised her. He was not, however, mocking her. "You know Mr. Pope's words well."

"I admire him," Phyllis responded. "I have read his 'Essay on Man' many times." In the background she could see Thomas Woolbridge smiling. He was perhaps the only member of the group not surprised by Phyllis' knowledge of one of the most important poems written during the century.

"Do you know his meaning as well as you do the words?" Byles asked.

"He is saying that we live in a divinely created and perfect order," Phyllis began. "All things have their place in that order. All creatures are a link in the chain. If one link breaks, no matter its place, the whole order is shattered."

Thomas Hubbard suddenly interjected himself into the dialogue. "And if a creature presumes to take a place other than the one God created for it?"

"The order is shattered," Phyllis responded.

"Exactly!" Hubbard exclaimed. "And that you, a Negro, would presume to change your place in the order would be destructive. Correct?"

Phyllis knew her response. She had had such similar conversations with Nathaniel that it was as if she had rehearsed this moment. And yet, staring into the eyes of the hostile Mr. Hubbard instead of the gentle gaze of Nathaniel, she froze. She understood the man's motivations. He saw her as an Abolitionist. She did not see herself as one. Abolitionists had social and political motivations. Phyllis was simply engaging in philosophical discussion. All she wanted to do was print a book of her poems.

"So," Hubbard continued, "the fact that you are here asking to be acknowledged as a poet contradicts the very ideals of the poet whom you claim to understand."

"God's peace, Thomas," Hancock exploded. "Clearly she does not claim to understand the man. She does understand him. You heard her." The room filled with mutters of agreement. No one particularly cared for Thomas Hubbard, though his importance as a man of business and politics could not be denied. Hubbard glared at the disagreeable Hancock.

"'Far as creation's ample range extends,/The scale of sensual, mental pow'rs ascends,'" Phyllis quoted further from Pope's work. The room grew quiet until Hubbard responded.

"Yes, you quote lines well. We are not here, however, to judge your ability to memorize poetry."

"Our place in the order is not determined by the color of our skin or our place of origin. Nor by our senses. It is determined by the power of our minds. That is what the poem is saying, I think."

"Gentlemen," Thomas Hutchinson said, exerting his power as governor. "I think I've heard enough." Again the room filled with words of agreement. Even the contentious Chauncy nodded his approval of the governor's words. Only Hubbard continued to glare.

"We will be with you shortly," Hutchinson said to Phyllis. As she left the room, she noticed the cat-like grin on Mr. Woolbridge's face. In the hallway, Phyllis rejoined Nathaniel. Her knees were weak. She had maintained her poise at a price. Now she felt faint and sick. Nathaniel took her hand and guided her to a chair. There they remained, unspeaking, until Woolbridge joined them and handed Nathaniel a formally, though hastily, prepared document. Nathaniel broke the seal and read it aloud:

> We whose Names are under-written, do assure the World, that the Poems specified in the following Page, were (as we verily believe) written by Phyllis, a young Negro Girl, who was but a few Years since, brought an uncultivated Barbarian from Africa, and has ever since been, and now is, under the Disadvantage of serving as a Slave in a Family in this Town. She has been examined by some of the best Judges, and is thought qualified to write them.

When Nathaniel handed the page to Phyllis to examine, two signatures stood out from the others. That of John Hancock was unusually large. And that of Thomas Hubbard, though not so distinctive, was, nonetheless, present.

* * *

At the same time Susanna was arranging for her book to be printed in London, Phyllis was suffering from the asthma which affected her throughout her life. The Wheatleys' doctor suggested that Phyllis might benefit from an ocean voyage that would expose her to salty sea air. With this thought in mind, John and Susanna Wheatley decided to send Phyllis to London with their son Nathaniel. There she could observe the final planning for her book and seek support for its publication. Phyllis and Nathaniel left Boston on May 8, 1773, aboard the Wheatleys' packet the London, a three-masted schooner captained by Robert Calef. For the first time since being bought by Susanna Wheatley, Phyllis was away from her mistress. The grief created by this separation, especially that felt by Susanna, is obvious in the poem Phyllis wrote on the occasion, "A Farewell to AMERICA, To Mrs. S. W.":

> Susannah mourns, nor can I bear
> To see the crystal show'r,
> Or mark the tender falling tear
> At sad departure's hour . . .
> Not unregarding can I see
> Her soul with grief opprest:
> But let no sighs, no groans for me,
> Steal from her pensive breast . . .

Phyllis carried with her, however, more than sadness. She was excited to taking such an adventure and one which presented its irony the moment that she stepped aboard ship. Her last ocean voyage, twelve years earlier, had brought her to Boston a slave, sick and in all likelihood about to die of sickness. This voyage would carry her to London, a celebrated figure in the literary world. Phyllis carried with her more than emotions, however. She took with her the dedication for her book, which read as follows:

TO
THE RIGHT HONORABLE, THE
COUNTESS OF HUNTINGDON,
THE FOLLOWING POEMS
ARE MOST RESPECTFULLY INSCRIBED,
BY HER MUCH OBLIGED, VERY HUMBLE,
AND DEVOTED SERVANT,
PHYLLIS WHEATLEY,
BOSTON, JUNE 12, 1773.

She also had a portrait of herself that would appear as an engraving at the front of her volume of poems. In it, she appears in humble dress, with her eyes turned upward as if seeking divine inspiration. Scholars have speculated that the portrait was painted by the slave Scipio Moorhead, owned by the Reverend John Moorhead. Susanna Wheatley knew of this painter's work, and Phyllis had even written a poem in which she suggests that her craft and that of the painter were alike:

To show the lab'ring bosom's deep intent,
And thought in living characters to paint,
When thy pencil did those beauties give,
And breathing figures learnt from thee to live,
How did those prospects give my soul delight,
A new creation rushing on my sight!
Still, wondrous youth! Each noble path pursue,
On deathless glories fix thine ardent view:
Still may the painter's and the poet's fire
To aid thy pencil and thy verse conspire!
And may the charms of each seraphic theme
Conduct thy footsteps to immortal fame!

The selection of a painter, however, would have been Susanna's duty. Given that a principal attraction of Phyllis' book was that it contained poems written by a slave, Susanna would have seen the added appeal of having the portrait of Phyllis also painted by a slave. Finally, Phyllis took with her to be included in the book the statement by the men from New England stating that the poems were in fact written by Phyllis Wheatley. Her book appeared in London in early summer 1773. The title was *Poems on Various Subjects, Religious and Moral*. In 1774, it became available in Nova Scotia and New England, just ahead of the British blockade of American ports. The final publication was an octavo volume containing 39 poems, many of them elegies. Phyllis decided, however, to omit the America poems from this book printed in England. Many of them dealt with the political conflict between England and the colonies. Phyllis had expressed in them her belief in the cause of freedom. Although Phyllis was a slave, with no legal claim to any income the book might produce, she did receive one half of the sales proceeds.

Chapter IV

Phyllis Wheatley in London

"What wonderful creatures," Phyllis cried as she and her friend Granville Sharp visited the Tower of London and looked at the African animals which were kept there.

"Animals from Africa, your home," Sharp responded. Phyllis did not react to her friend's comment. She had heard him make the same point in various ways and on many occasions since their first meeting shortly after she had arrived in London. Instead, she allowed her gaze to move from the area where the towering elephants moved contentedly to cages that held monkeys which played frantically on the large tree limbs that had been arranged into a tangled configuration. "You are as captive as those animals," Sharp added.

Phyllis could only look at her new friend. She understood that Sharp wanted her to accept her African background. He had been constantly reminding her for days that she was not an American either by birth or by race. He was as adamant about the issue of slavery as she was about her own beliefs.

Sharp had gone with Phyllis to see not only the Tower of London, but also the British Museum, Greenwich, and Westminster Abbey. There Phyllis had marveled not so much at the magnificence of the cathedral. What had amazed her was seeing the memorials to famous men and the members of England's royalty. That she would actually stand beside the tomb of the kings and queens who had shaped that country's history thrilled Phyllis. And ever at her side was the insistent Granville Sharp. No matter what he said, however, Phyllis' response was always the same.

"Tower of London" on the   Páiraig Michael Mann 1/11/2006

"My home is Boston."

"Phyllis, you are an African," Sharp said. He did not give up easily. Yet, dressed in the clothing of an English gentleman, Sharp did not himself present the image of an African. Phyllis smiled as if the contrast between her companion's appearance and his words had occurred to her. She would never have spoken such thoughts, however. She admired Sharp's passion. Phyllis appreciated his friendship. He did not treat her as if she were some oddity. As kind as other Londoners might be, Phyllis was always aware that their interest in her was not based on her character. They wanted to examine this marvel, this black woman who could write poetry and discuss philosophy. Sharp, on the other hand, might admire her work, but did not see her as in any way a contradiction to the natural order of things. For him, she was not an oddity as she was to so many of the people she had been meeting. Phyllis was happy to have such a companion.

Sharp did not see her as some sort of aberration because of her abilities. He did, however, see her as proof that his efforts to secure political equality for Negroes was based on their actually being as capable as whites in all aspects of life, including scholarly and creative pursuits. Phyllis needed time with such a man to keep from feeling like a kindly regarded freak.

"I was born in Africa," Phyllis said, "but remember nothing of my life there. Except for a vague image of my mother the morning before I was taken captive. But you know how I feel. The Wheatleys have been kind to me."

"They keep you a slave," Sharp said quickly.

"But they treat me like a member of the family. Please understand. What matters to me is what they think of me. And you, Granville . . . what you think. That does matter to me, as well."

Sharp nodded. Once again, Phyllis had shown her loyalty to the Wheatleys.

"And," she then added, "I thank you for being my friend. I do respect your feelings."

Sharp smiled. It was a small victory in their ongoing debate. But a victory he was willing to accept. He admired Phyllis, but also liked her and valued their friendship too much to push her too severely on the slavery issue.

It was not that Phyllis did not acknowledge her African heritage. In many of her poems, she referred to herself as having been brought from Africa as a slave. In "America," a poem written much later in her life, she drew a parallel between her enslavement and that which the colonies suffered at the hands of British rule. But she had almost no memories of her life before going to live with the Wheatleys. What she did remember is how Wheatleys had treated her with a kindness that slaves rarely experienced, even in their household. They had bought her when she was seriously ill and helped her regain her health. Boston was her home. She was never in doubt about the fact. She did not feel, however, that by saying this she was being disloyal to her race or her beliefs.

Sharp, on the other hand, was a freed African who had been important in the British Abolitionist movement. He had helped when the British Parliament had passed a law which said that slaves who touched British soil were free. According to that law, they could not be forced to return to their masters. Phyllis was in essence a freed woman, if she had chosen to exercise her rights according to British law.

Nathaniel Wheatley had even been concerned about this law and the influence that Sharp might have on Phyllis once they arrived in London. He had accompanied Phyllis primarily because she had been in poor health before leaving and he was at the time of their departure a physician. His father had, however, also felt that Nathaniel should accompany Phyllis to protect the family's interest in her and in her growing fame. Phyllis was not swayed by the response her being a slave caused in London. Nor did she give any indication that she thought of herself as being free after reaching England. Many of the magazines which wrote of her visit to London and reviewed her book spoke harshly about her remaining enslaved. The writers took particular note of the ideals of freedom that were being expressed in the colonies. They questioned American accusations of British dictatorship while still practicing slavery. How, these writers would ask, could a people so concerned with freedom continue the practice of slavery? Phyllis, however, did not enter into this debate while in London. Rather, she used her time there to meet several famous people, including Benjamin

Franklin. When he heard Phyllis was in London, Franklin asked for and received permission to call on Phyllis during her stay. Her only other concern was with the publication of her book, and Phyllis worked diligently to make sure that it correctly presented her poetry.

Phyllis also had the chance to meet the Earl of Dartmouth. She had written a poem to this gentleman when he served as Secretary of State for the Colonies and President of the Board of Trade and Foreign Plantations. The poem praised Dartmouth's efforts at ending British taxation of the colonies. In it, Phyllis wrote one of her most direct references to her own enslavement:

Should you, my lord, while you peruse my song,
Wonder from whence my love of Freedom sprung,
Whence flow these wishes for the common good,
By feeling hearts alone best understood,—
I, young in life, by seeming cruel fate
Was snatched from Africa's fancied happy seat:
What pangs excruciating must molest,
What sorrows labour in my parent's breast!

Writers in England enjoyed pointing out the injustice of a freedom-loving people, as the American colonists claimed to be, practicing slavery. They used Phyllis as an example of the absurdity of the situation and her achievements as evidence that Negroes were not of an inferior race. In article after article British journalists alluded to the ironic connection between the practice of slavery and the political issues of the day. Phyllis was well aware of this irony. Even in her poem to Dartmouth, however, Phyllis referred to the "fate" that cost her her freedom as "seeming cruel," not "being" cruel. In this choice of words she reflects her feeling that being brought to America cost her her freedom, but saved her soul because of bringing her to a Christian nation. She closed her poem "On Being Brought from Africa to America" with the following lines:

Remember, Christians, Negroes black as Cain
May be refined, and join the angelic train.

The primary thrust of these lines is to make clear that Africans were also God's children and could be saved. The poem does indicate that that salvation would not be possible living in the heretical culture of their native land.

Dartmouth was pleased with the words Phyllis spoke of him. When the two met in London, he repaid her with a gift she truly valued, books. She received Tobias Smollet's 1775 translation of Cervantes' Don Quixote, John Gay's Fables, Samuel Butler's Hudibras, and Alexander Pope's translation of the epics of the Greek poet Homer. These books, along with the copy of a folio edition of John Milton's poetry given to her by the merchant Brook Watson, who later became Lord Mayor of London, were treasures for the young writer.

A few days after visiting the Tower of London with Granville Sharp, Phyllis was sitting quietly in her London room. She heard a soft knock on the door.

"Nathaniel," Phyllis whispered when she opened the door and saw the look on the face which greeted her. "What is it?"

"Mother, Phyllis. I just received word she is ill."

Phyllis hesitated only a moment and then moved to begin packing her things. Her modest lifestyle was such that she needed only minutes to organize herself.

"What are you doing?" Nathaniel asked.

"I must return home. Can you help me find passage?"

"We'll take our ship. I'm going as well. But it will take a few days to prepare the ship for travel. No reason to pack tonight." Nathaniel managed a weak smile. Phyllis did not.

Unfortunately for Phyllis, her arrival in London during the summer limited her social opportunities. Her patron, the Countess of Huntingdon, was in southern Wales at the time. Also, the young King George III was away from the city. Had she been able to remain in London until the social season began in the fall, she would have had the chance to meet both. However, after hearing of Susanna Wheatley's illness, she immediately made plans to return to Boston and left on July 7, 1773, approximately five weeks after her arrival.

* * *

Susanna Wheatley had grown frail by the early autumn of 1773 and spent most of her time confined to her bed. There, at Susanna's bedside Phyllis remained, her constant companion and her nurse. Their roles had reversed. Thirteen years earlier, Susanna had attended to Phyllis and pulled her back from death. Now, though, the result would not be the same. Phyllis did all that she could to make her mistress comfortable. On those days when Susanna seemed to have a bit of strength, Phyllis had directed Prince to help Susanna to the small sitting area in the yard behind their house. There they could enjoy the bright colors of the leaves as they turned to their autumn gold and red.

On one of those days when Phyllis and Susanna were sitting together, Nathaniel approached carrying a packet. He first bent to give his smiling mother a kiss and then looked at Phyllis.

"Are you ready to discover your fame in London?" Phyllis squinted as if by adjusting her eyes she might be better able to understand Nathaniel's comment. "Calef has just returned from his latest trip to London." Nathaniel thrust a packet at Phyllis. "He has brought copies of the publications in London which have spoken of your book."

Phyllis eagerly reached for the packet and then stopped, setting it in her lap.

"What's wrong, Phyllis?" Susanna asked with a small voice. Though her eyes were smiling and expectant, her frailty did not allow her to react with the zeal that she felt in her heart.

"Have you looked?" Phyllis asked, looking into Nathaniel's eyes to see if she could see some indication of what she should expect.

Nathaniel laughed. "The package isn't addressed to me."

"Then you don't know what they say? Did Mr. Calef . . . ?"

Nathaniel laughed again and took his seat on a small stone bench. As he shook his head, Phyllis turned her eyes to the package that lay in her lap. Earlier in the summer she had received copies of her book, although it was not yet available to buy in the colonies. She had held the book as if it were a bird, so softly that if she were to squeeze, something terrible would result. The package that lay in her lap she treated more like a colorful serpent. She looked at it with wonder, but seemed reluctant to touch, much less open, it to see what was inside.

"Phyllis," Susanna said quietly. "I am sure that you will not be disappointed."

Phyllis smiled. As was so often the case, she felt put at ease by Susanna's kindness. As her long fingers began to tear at the edges of the package, Phyllis was shaking. She had had to prove herself in front of great men in both Boston and London, and been successful. On all these occasions, she had felt uncomfortable, as she did facing the packet of reviews of her book.

Phyllis slipped out the first of the journals. Its title caused her to wince: *Critical Review*. She thumbed its pages until she found the piece that referred to her work.

After a few moments of allowing Phyllis to read, Susanna spoke up. "What does it say, Phyllis?"

Phyllis shook her head and then read, "The Negroes of Africa are generally treated as a dull ignorant, and ignoble race of men, fit only to be slaves, and incapable of any considerable attainments in the liberal arts and sciences. A poet or poetess amongst them, of any tolerable genius, would be a prodigy in literature. Phyllis Wheatley, the author of these poems, is this literary phenomenon." Phyllis stopped and looked up to the expectant faces of Susanna and Nathaniel.

"Is that all?" Nathaniel said, the smile leaving his face. Phyllis shook her head. "What else?"

Phyllis began again. "The pieces, of which this little volume consists, are the productions of her leisure moments. And though they are not remarkably beautiful, they have too much merit to be thrown aside, as trifling and worthless effusions."

Susanna lifted herself as best she could. "I think this is not bad, Phyllis. We would have preferred a more appreciative reader, but he does acknowledge you." Nathaniel nodded his agreement.

"I am an oddity, not an artist."

"No, Phyllis, you are a gifted poet," Susanna interjected quickly.

"I do not write in my 'leisure time.' I work at my writing," Phyllis said with enough anger in her voice to concern Susanna and Nathaniel.

"Is that the end of the review?" Nathaniel asked.

"I didn't read further," Phyllis said as she turned her eyes back to the pages that lay in front of her. When she began again, the words came with increasing difficulty. "There are several lines in this piece...It is talking about 'To Maecenas.' There are several lines in this piece which would be no discredit to an English poet. The whole is indeed extraordinary . . . considered . . . as the production of a young Negro." Phyllis broke off, now tears crawling down her face.

"Phyllis," Susanna Wheatley said firmly. "They don't know how to speak of your work. The British have freed their slaves, but they haven't yet learned how to view Africans. That is why the article keeps going back to that idea."

"Exactly," Nathaniel added. "I think that writer admires your work, but just doesn't know how to present that admiration. Mother is exactly right."

Phyllis smiled as she placed the journal back in the packet.

"There are others, Phyllis," Nathaniel said. "Let's have a look." Phyllis handed him the packet and watched as he removed the entire contents and began looking at the reviews of Phyllis' book. Slowly his expression changed from anticipation to sadness. Then as he pinched his lips and his eyes grew dark, Phyllis knew that there was a rage in Nathaniel. Susanna saw it as well.

"Calef didn't bother to read this rubbish," Nathaniel said abruptly. He never would have sent it to us otherwise.

"I want to see," Phyllis said.

"There is nothing here fit to read."

"Nathaniel, you brought this to me, for my use. Please"

Reluctantly, Nathaniel handed the scorching pages back to Phyllis, who received them as if they were hot coals pulled from the stove.

"Read to me, Phyllis," Susanna said, "and don't you mind the words. We will read it and then that will be that."

Phyllis began tentatively as tears again began to form in her eyes. She was looking at a journal entitled *Monthly Review*. "If we believed, with the ancient mythologists, that genius is the offspring of the sun, we should rather wonder that the sable race have not been more distinguished by it, than express our surprise at a single instance. The poems written by this young negro bear no . . . bear no . . . no endemial marks of solar fire or spirit. They . . . are . . . merely imitative; . . . and, indeed, most of those people have a turn for imitation, though they have little or none for invention." When she had finished, Phyllis was weeping openly. Nathaniel was pacing back and forth, his hands on his hips and his range unabated. Susanna remained pensive.

"But what just makes me furious," Nathaniel said suddenly, "is that the people who wrote that rubbish attack us in the colonies for keeping slaves. There is more contempt for Negroes in those words. Wait. Phyllis, may I have the other one." Phyllis looked at Nathaniel. Her tears had begun to dry.

"Miss Susanna doesn't need to hear that."

"Hear what?" Susanna asked.

"Listen to this," Nathaniel said as he reached with obvious demand for the copy of Gentleman's Magazine which had been included in the package. Listen, mother. "Youth, innocence, and piety, united with genius, have not yet been able to restore her to the condition and character with which she was invested by the Great Author of her being. So powerful is custom in rendering the heart insensible to the rights of nature, and the claims of excellence!" Nathaniel stopped.

"Nathaniel," Susanna said quietly as Phyllis, now free of tears, observed her mistress. "You missed the important point in those words. Yes, they are attacking us because Phyllis is a slave."

"But mother we treat her…"

"Nathaniel! And we should be mindful of our shortcomings. Not aggressive in pointing out our virtues. But the important word there is 'genius.' Phyllis, the reviewer referred to you with the word 'genius.'"

Nathaniel's jaw dropped, and Phyllis turned an attentive eye to Susanna. Susanna was smiling, but she was growing pale. She needed to rest.

"Nathaniel," Susanna said, "you help me to my room. Phyllis, would you join me for a cup of tea? I'd like to be in the company of a genius this afternoon!"

* * *

Phyllis' decision to return to Boston quickly had been wise, for Susanna Wheatley lived less than a year, not even long enough to see *Poems on Various Subjects, Religious and Moral* released in the colonies. Just as it had in London, the book received mixed reactions at home. When it became available in the colonies, John Paul Jones sent one of his officers to purchase a copy for him. Another notable American had a response to Phyllis' writing. Specifically, Thomas Jefferson said, "Religion, indeed, has produced a Phyllis Wheatley, but it could not produce a poet." Phyllis was never aware of either man's reaction. She would have in all likelihood not cared what they thought if she had known. When the book appeared in the colonies, she was still mourning the passing of Susanna Wheatley and contending with serious changes in her own life.

Chapter V

Freedom

While Phyllis Wheatley was in London, she could not avoid the discussions about her being forced to continue her life as a slave. Granville Sharp's words on the subject were the product of his political and social thinking. He had developed a fondness for Phyllis that made him want her to consider the options she had in her life that might bring her happiness. The magazines that discussed the reception of this unique literary figure and later reviewed her book would raise the slavery question repeatedly. No one, none of the jounralists, doubted that she was well treated by the Wheatleys. The issue was that Phyllis Wheatley was not free even though her masters seemed to appreciate her unique abilities. The Wheatleys were often characterized as people who wanted to present Phyllis as they would a unique possession, not a talented human being. Phyllis' response was always the same. Just as she told Granville Sharp, she was content with her life and appreciative of the treatment she had always received from John and Susanna Wheatley. In July 1773, Phyllis' only concern, despite how much she was enjoying London, was caring for Susanna.

The Wheatleys, however, were aware of the criticism of their keeping Phyllis in slavery. In January 1774, six months after Phyllis returned from London, she was manumitted by John Wheatley. Her freedom did not, however, alter Phyllis' devotion to Susanna Wheatley. She continued to attend to her needs until Susanna died March 3, 1774. The passing of her mistress left Phyllis with an enormous dispair, but also an opportunity. Any moral obligation she might have felt to remain with the Wheatleys was gone. Nathaniel and

Mary were adults living on their own. Susanna's passing left Phyllis with no function really. She could well have left and pursued one of the many opportunities that had been presented to her during her brief stay in London.

While in London, Phyllis had met John Thornton, a devoted clergyman and Abolitionist. The literary skills and Christian beliefs of the young poet had impressed him greatly. He continued to write letters to Phyllis after her return to Boston. Upon learning that she had been freed, he asked Phyllis to return to Africa with other former slaves who had become ministers and seek converts to the Christian faith. Such an offer must have tempted Phyllis, given her belief that the one thing that Africans should be grateful for about being taken into slavery was that it brought them the salvation of Christianity. Thornton offered her the chance to take that gift directly to Africa. Phyllis, however, chose to remain in Boston, to serve her role as a servant in the Wheatley household, and to pursue her literary career.

During these years, Phyllis maintained her interest in the cause of American freedom. She had, in fact, been attentive to the major events that had occurred in Boston, often near the Wheatley home, that had already taken place. In February 1770, Ebenezer Richardson, a Boston Tory who supported King George's decision to send British troops to Boston, was faced with a protesting mob in front of his house. When the mob began throwing snowballs through his windows, Richardson fired into the crowd. The shot killed eleven-year-old Christopher Snyder. This event had prompted Phyllis to write one of her earliest poems on the growing political tension in the colonies. In that poem, "On the Death of Mr. Snider Murder'd by Richardson," she described Snyder as the "first martyr for the cause." That Phyllis saw that there was a "cause" is significant because she wrote this poem years before the colonies declared their independence. She was able to see, however, that the "cause" of freedom was beginning to shape the colonists' thoughts. Her evaluation would have been confirmed almost immediately, for in the same year that Christopher Snyder was killed, the city experienced, again very near the Wheatley home, what has come to be known as the Boston Massacre. A British soldier guarding the city customs house hit a young man with his rifle in response to a shouted insult. A crowd gathered to include between three and four hundred men. The tension grew, and when the mob finally assaulted the soldier first involved in the event, he and other British guards began to fire on the crowd. Left lying in the streets five men lay dead, and six were wounded. One of those slain was Crispus Attacus, a former slave who had fled captivity and been living as a free man. Then, in 1773, while Phyllis was enjoying the fruits of being a published poet, she would have experienced as well the events known as the Boston Tea Party. The colonists resented the excessive taxation which the British levied against them. The Stamp Act had generated considerable anger. When, however, the colonists were faced with a heavy tax on tea, their patience was severely tested. A number of colonists marched on Boston Harbor dressed as native Americans and dumped more that three hundred chests of tea into the ocean. This act led the British to close Boston Harbor and to place the colony's government completely under the King's rule. Her correspondence reveals that Phyllis wrote on these events as well as the occasional poem she wrote about the death of Christopher Snyder. However, in order to secure a British publisher, Phyllis had to remove from her manuscript many of her "America" poems. Many of these have been lost. One poem about her quest for freedom which has survived is that which Phyllis wrote about and dedicated to George Washington. She wrote the following lines in her poem "To His Excellency General Washington":

Thee, first in peace and honours,—we demand
The grace and glory of thy martial band,
Fam'd for thy valour, for thy virtues more,
Hear every tongue that guardian aid implore!

Phyllis sent a copy of this poem to Washington and enclosed a letter explaining her desire to celebrate his "being appointed by the Grand Continental Congress to be Generalissimo of the armies of North America." Washington would later make arrangements for the poem to be published in the March 1776 edition of the Virginia Gazette.

Washington also sent a response to Phyllis. In it, he apologized for the fact that his letter of thanks was so late, pleading the demanding schedule of his duties. He closed the letter with an invitation: "If you should ever come to Cambridge, or near headquarters, I shall be happy to see a person so favored by the Muses, and to whom nature has been so liberal and beneficent in her dispensations. I am, with great respect, your obedient humble servant."

* * *

Phyllis arrived at the encampment where Washington had established his headquarters with a greater sense of awe than she had ever experienced before on any other such occasion. She had met great men. She had faced the inquisition of Massachusetts' leading political and religious figures to establish her authorship of the poems she proposed to publish under her name. She had been visited by Benjamin Franklin while in London and met other distinguished persons, including the future Lord Mayor of London. Washington, however, was not simply a man of position. He was one devoted to the cause of freedom which Phyllis had embraced. Her enthusiasm is interesting, for the lack of concern she appears to have had for her individual freedom contrasts with the passion which she felt for the cause of American liberty. General Washington may have referred in his letter to being Phyllis' "obedient humble servant," but she understood that this was the protocol wording used by gentlemen at the end of a letter. She refused to view Washington as anything less than the great man, passionate patriot, and distinguished leader that he was. Nonetheless, Phyllis had received a formal invitation from the general and was determined as both a matter of social obligation and genuine personal interest to accept his offer.

"Miss Phyllis," General Washington said after seeing the young black woman who had entered his tent at his headquarters near Cambridge. Washington bowed slightly. Phyllis returned with the curtsey she had perfected during her visit to London. She was awed by the greatness of the man she had been invited to visit. He stood tall, dressed in a splendid uniform. His kind face was framed by the white powdered wig that he wore on all occasions.

"It is an honor to meet such a fine writer."

"Thank you, sir," was all Phyllis could manage to say.

Washington approached and stepped past the officer who had brought Phyllis to his tent but not known how to introduce the general to a black woman and former slave.

"And I thank you for the kind words you wrote about me!"

"I am honored by your invitation to visit," Phyllis finally managed to utter. The easy manner of this great man was quickly putting her at ease.

"Please," Washington said, "can you sit a few minutes and tell me about your poetry?" How could this busy general take time to visit with her about poetry? Phyllis was delighted to have the chance! She took the seat that Washington offered and sat quietly as he pulled up his own chair. They provided an interesting contrast. The large and dynamic white general and the frail, modest black woman. The military genius and the artistic prodigy. The farmer and slave owner and the recently freed slave.

"I fear, Miss Phyllis, I have had little occasion to read your work, but understand that you have published a volume of verse."

"Yes," Phyllis replied. For the second time in her life she had been addressed formally by a distinguished gentleman. As with the first occasion, she was somewhat startled. "My late mistress, Mrs. Wheatley, made the arrangements."

"I see," Washington nodded. "But I am to understand that you are now free?"

"Yes sir. But I still live in the Wheatley home."

"And you said your late mistress?"

"Mrs. Wheatley died two years ago, sir."

Washington observed Phyllis. Her voice softened when she spoke of Susanna's passing.

"May I offer you tea?" Washington asked suddenly, and Phyllis smiled her appreciation. Washington looked back at his aide who had escorted Phyllis earlier. The officer understood the general's desire and left promptly.

"I can see that she was dear to you."

"Yes sir. Mrs. Wheatley bought me when I was a child. I was poorly, but she took me home."

"And did she encourage you to learn to read and to write? You say that she arranged the publishing of your poems?"

"Yes sir. Her daughter, Miss Mary, taught me."

Washington nodded. "It is a rare thing for a woman. Especially for a slave."

"The Wheatleys never treated me like a slave," Phyllis said quickly.

Again Washington nodded. The demands of his duty and his interest in spending time with this remarkable woman conflicted.

"Not all slaves are so lucky," he observed after a pause. "I have been told that there are 700,000 slaves in the colonies, maybe more. I am sure that very few have lived a life such as yours."

"Yes sir," Phyllis said.

"We have struggles ahead, Miss Phyllis, if we are going to learn the true nature of freedom . . . and its proper scope. Well, tell me, which authors do you read?"

Phyllis' visit with Washington lasted thirty minutes. She either left no real record of the occasion, or else anything she did write has been lost. Sadly, Phyllis' life would quickly begin to change, and her days of visiting with great men and discussing with them important ideas were over.

Within two years of her meeting with Washington, Phyllis' life changed dramatically. In 1778, John Wheatley died at age 72. Phyllis still had a home with the tutor of her youth, Mary Wheatly Lathrop. Mary's husband John was a distinguished and successful minister in Massachusetts. However, in that same year, Mary died as well. Just as she had nursed her mother, Phyllis attended to Mary, the tutor who had been much like a sister to her. Mary had given birth to five children in less than five years. She had seen only one of those children survive, and finally her body and spirit failed. Neither she nor her father left Phyllis anything in their estates, nor did Nathaniel Wheatley who died in London in 1783. In 1778, Phyllis Wheatley was freed, but she was without home or livelihood. After Wheatley's death, Phyllis stayed briefly with a family friend and then found her own apartment. She was, however, in poor position to support herself.

* * *

"I've been your friend a long time, Phyllis," Obdour Tanner said as she placed a steaming cup of tea in front of her companion. They were sitting quietly in the kitchen of James Tanner's home in Newport, Rhode Island. Her words spoke the obvious. Obdour and Phyllis were the same age. They had met when still very young when the Wheatleys had visited Newport, a popular vacation area for Boston residents. Like Phyllis, Obdour had received much kinder treatment from her owner than slaves generally received. She, too, had been allowed an education. As a result, Obdour and Phyllis had remained close by writing letters back and forth. In those letters, they had developed the habit of referring to each other as "dear sister." They were, in fact, as close to being sisters as they could have been without being of the same family. As Obdour poured her own cup of tea and then sat across the table from her friend, Phyllis could see the price she had paid as a result of poor health. While she was small—framed and frail, Obdour was healthy and robust. Phyllis' cheeks were hollow; Obdour's full and robust. The two of them looked to Phyllis as if years separated them in age, not weeks or months. They could not be sure exactly because neither knew her birthday. "You may not like what I have to say. But you will not be doing yourself proper by marrying John Peters."

Phyllis drew herself up in her chair and pinched her eyes. Obdour did not respond to Phyllis' physical reaction. Instead, she stared her friend even more directly in the eyes.

"John is a good man," Phyllis said after a few moments.

"He thinks himself more than he is," Obdour responded. "Calling himself Doctor Peters. That man is no doctor."

"Well," Phyllis said as she lifted the cup to her mouth and blew gently before taking a sip of the tea. Again the two women fell silent and let the quiet cut the edge from the tension both were feeling.

Phyllis and Obdour had both known John Peters since they were teenagers. He was a freed slave who made his way in the world in whatever way he could manage. As a young man, he had earned his living running errands and doing odd jobs. One of these was to serve as a courier for those members of New England society who could afford such services, including James Tanner and John Wheatley. He had carried letters between Phyllis and Obdour and had taken the occasions when he saw them to visit and make himself seem an agreeable companion. Peters liked Phyllis and had followed her literary career with great interest. Phyllis had once referred to him in a letter to Obdour as "complaisant and agreeable." Obdour had responded by saying that he "strutted like a bantam rooster." Phyllis had laughed at the time. More than ten years later, each held basically the same opinion that they had expressed in their youth. Peters, however, had visited Phyllis after the death of John Wheatley and asked her to be his wife. Phyllis had not given him an answer, but he had returned to her a second time, and then a third. Phyllis knew that she must Tell Peters her decision and had decided to confide in Obdour.

"That man's interest in you is not what you think," Obdour said fiercely.

"What do you mean?" Phyllis asked.

"You be angry with me if you want. But he likes that you are famous."

"I'm not famous," Phyllis said. Her eyes did not darken, but she chose not to look at Obdour and show that her feelings were hurt.

Obdour shrugged. "You published a book of your poetry. You met General Washington. You been to London."

"That was in the past," Philis said. "Now that the Wheatleys are gone, nobody cares about me." Phyllis paused, "Except you, Obdour." The warmth in the words encouraged Obdour that she had not over stepped herself by being so direct with her friend.

"There's lots of folks still know who you are and care about you. John Peters knows that."

"He never talks about my writing."

"He's too busy talking about himself, I 'spect," Obdour smiled. Phyllis returned the smile.

"He's an interesting man," Phyllis responded.

"He's interesting all right. Walking 'round with that white wig and carrying that cane. He's just what I told you a long time ago. He's a strutting bantam rooster."

Phyllis wanted to laugh. She knew that Obdour was right in her assessment of John Peters. Phyllis, however, did not mind John Peters' ways. "He's not like those men I met in London. They were like roosters with their fancy clothes and even powder on their faces and such."

"Well," Obdour said. "He's a rooster from the colonies. They were roosters from London. But it doesn't matter. They both roosters."

Finally, Phyllis had to laugh. She remembered seeing the men in London who were so well dressed and whose manners were so different from what she had grown accustomed to in colonial New England. Obdour was seeing John Peters the way she had seen them. Despite the humor the two women were finding, Phyllis knew that she had a serious decision to make. She had not come to Obdour for her blessing, but to help her sort through her own thoughts. Phyllis pinched her eyes again.

"What?" Obdour asked, reading her friend's expression.

"Seems so long ago that I was in London meeting all those people. So much has happened." Obdour nodded. Much had happened, not just to Phyllis but to everyone as the colonies had demanded freedom from British oppression and gone to war to achieve that end.

"That man doesn't go to church, does he?" Obdour asked, deciding to try a different approach.

Phyllis looked down. She took up a spoon and began to stir her tea even though she had added no milk or sugar. For a few moments, the only sound was the clicking of the spoon against the side of the cup. "No."

"How are you going to marry a man that doesn't believe the way you do?"

"I think if I tell him it is important to me he will change."

Obdour shook her head. Now she was staring into her cup as if she might find an answer to Phyllis' questions somehow sitting in the light brown liquid.

"What?" Phyllis asked.

"I don't think you best expect a man to change just because you want him to. He is what he is."

"If he loves me the way he says, he will," Phyllis snapped. She loved Obdour but was beginning to feel that their discussion was serving no purpose.

"That's what I've been saying. That man wants to marry you because you are important. I'm sorry, but that's the way I see things." Phyllis did not respond, and again the room grew quiet.

"Obdour, I am alone," Phyllis whispered.

The look in her friend's eyes told Phyllis that she wanted to disagree, but Obdour knew the truth. Phyllis was alone. She had received no consideration in the wills left by John Wheatley nor his daughter, Mary, who had been Phyllis' teacher so many years ago. Mary had, in fact, been the first person to discover Phyllis' talents. And Phyllis had nursed Mary through her own illness. Phyllis had been well-treated and loved while Susanna was alive. She had been freed, but allowed to remain as a member of the Wheatley household after her death. Yet, no provision had been made for her that would last beyond John Wheatley's passing. Phyllis was on her own. The money she had received from her book several years earlier was quickly gone once she had to care for herself. Her poor health was a serious concern. Also, because Phyllis had never really been expected to do anything except pursue her art, she had no skills. She could read and write. She knew the Bible as well as the most learned seminary student. She could wrestle with complex philosophical questions. She had even debated philosophy with distinguished and well-educated gentlemen. None of that, however, served her needs now. None of her accomplishments qualified her for a position which would enable her to earn her keep. A black woman, a freed slave, would be admired for being able to do the things Phyllis could do. Such a woman, however, would not be given a position which required her skills. Not only was Phyllis alone, she was without means or the ability to make her way in the world.

"I know," Obdour said after a moment. "But I want you to consider. Will John Peters be able to provide for you? Will he want children? Will your health allow you to have children? There's so much, Phyllis."

Phyllis nodded. She had already thought about the very things that Obdour was mentioning. Those very same thoughts had caused Phyllis to not immediately accept Peters' proposal. The time had arrived, however, for her to find answers.

* * *

On April 1, 1778, and despite the objections of Obour Tanner, Phyllis married John Peters. Phyllis had known Peters, himself a freed slave, for several years. Peters was an atypical figure, especially for a black man living in the colonies. He considered himself a refined gentleman. He wore a wig and carried a cane. He called himself Doctor Peters. He tried to practice law, especially to help freed slaves, but was better known as a grocer, baker, and barber. At first, Phyllis' marriage served her well. She and her husband lived in a house on Queen Street, which indicates that they had sufficient financial resources to buy property in one of Boston's affluent areas. Ultimately, however, though outgoing and smart, Peters was nonetheless unsuccessful at his various professions. And the times did not help the struggling new family. Boston was at the center of the military conflict that intensified in 1776 with the colonies' declaration of their independence. By 1778, Boston was at the center of the military conflict. To avoid this chaos, John and Phyllis Peters moved briefly to Wilmington, Massachusetts. Soon, however, British troops moved from the Boston area and Phyllis returned with her husband.

* * *

John Peters walked through the door of the small apartment he and Phyllis occupied and stepped to the stove. Phyllis had kept a small fire burning. She could see that her husband had not been successful with his efforts during the morning. How different he looked than he had only a few years ago when they had first married. Gone was the white wig which he had worn and which had framed his handsome features and allowed his dark eyes to command a room. Months ago he had sold the cane which he had twirled as he walked for the few coins it had brought. He had never needed the cane. It had simply accented his image as a distinguished and educated man. It had fit him when he had been known as Doctor Peters. John Peters had not needed a cane; in fact he had walked with a gait of confidence and strength. Now, he shuffled. His eyes were dark from hours of worry and long nights of lost sleep. John Peters was in debt. His grocery store had failed, as had the barber shop he had run for a time, at first with considerable success. His career representing freed slaves in the legal affairs they faced in their new lives, but about which they knew nothing, had ended. The colonies had gone to war, and such services were no longer in demand. The colonists, including the Negroes, freed and slave alike, had other business that needed attention.

Phyllis and her husband had lived on Queen Street in a prosperous part of Boston when they had first married. Now they lived amid the poverty of that part of the city where other freed slaves had created a community of their own. It was a poor area, kept poor by the effects of war and by the limited opportunities these Negroes had in the changing culture of the colonies. To escape the turmoil of war, Phyllis and John had lived in Wilmington briefly and made their way rather well. Their return to Boston after the British troops had left had, however, proved a greater test than either had anticipated. For a time, John Peters had been able to secure a license to sell liquor and made enough money at a little shop on Prince Street to support his family. He had, however, been accused of misrepresenting himself when he applied for that license. When he came in from seeing a city official about keeping his right to sell alcohol, Phyllis could see that his effort had failed.

Phyllis, too, had suffered serious losses as their lifestyle changed. Her health continued to be a problem. Living in the damp and chill of Massachusetts winters added to her difficulty. She had lost her first child shortly after his birth and was now pregnant with her second. She allowed her own struggle to fade from her mind, however, as she waited for her husband to tell her the news she already knew. Peters simply stood next to the stove and warmed his hands. When he did finally look at Phyllis, she saw an emptiness in his expression that caused her heart to sink.

"That family, the Wheatleys, they should have done for you," Peters said. Phyllis chose not to respond. She had heard the same assertion more often than she cared to remember. "All you did for them, and they left you with nothing."

As much as she hated to admit it, Phyllis felt there was truth in her husband's observations. That she had been treated well for a slave was without question. That Susanna Wheatley loved her, she did not doubt. Nor did Phyllis question whether she would have received greater consideration had Susanna outlived her husband. It was John Wheatley's decision not to include Phyllis in his will. But John Wheatley had always obviously tolerated his wife's treatment of Phyllis, but never felt as Susanna did about the little slave they had bought for what he once called a "trifle." It hurt Phyllis more that Mary had also passed over her at the time of her death. Even with a surviving husband and child, Mary could have left her a keepsake. But there had been nothing. Phyllis had received many gifts as a result of being a slave in the Wheatley home. None were of a nature that enabled her to survive as a free woman.

"I want you to gather your books for me," John Peters said after a while. Phyllis' eyes flashed as she knew immediately what her husband intended. She shook her head violently. "I have to have them, Phyllis."

"You are not going to sell my books."

"I don't have a choice. They are all we got left to sell."

"Those were gifts," Phyllis argued as she walked to face her husband. "There has to be another way."

Peters had spent the morning angered by his loss of his license to sell liquor. That anger was feeding his emotions as his wife, like the city official, was denying him his request. "I don't have another cane. Don't have a wig. Don't have anything more of mine I can sell, Phyllis." Peters' words spoke true. He had sold his own personal possessions already. But Phyllis was not ready to part with her books. And suddenly, Obdour's words returned to her. "That man wants you to take care of him." In little ways, ever since they had married, John Peters had proven Obdour had been right in her assessment of him. He had boasted his wife's fame to everyone they met. He had used her reputation to enhance his own position whenever possible. He had even used his wife when he had applied for his license to sell liquor. Now, finally, John Peters was asking for her most precious gifts. Her books were her last reminders of a life much different from the one she now led. And he was going to sell them.

"No," Phyllis said.

"You can't tell me no," Peters responded. As he spoke he added wood to the stove as if to say that anything they owned was his. He was going to put a piece of wood to the fire even though they were so poor that he was going to sell Phyllis' books.

"I did tell you no," Phyllis responded.

"Whatever is yours is mine. A wife doesn't say no to her husband. You'll find that in your Bible."

"A man honors and loves his wife. That is what I find in the Bible," Phyllis said. Even more than the fact that he intended to sell her books, John Peter's mocking her religious beliefs angered Phyllis. John Peters never read the Bible. He did not attend services with her. She had accepted the fact that he did not burn with the passion of religion as she did. But for him to mock her beliefs caused Phyllis to resent even more his demanding from her the books she cherished.

Peters stared at his wife. His shoulders sank. "They are going to put me in debtor's prison."

Phyllis knew that she and her husband were without money. She had no idea that he had borrowed money. "How?"

"I had to borrow money to get that shop I've been working. I didn't make enough to pay it back."

"When? How much?" Phyllis asked.

"I owe a lot of money. But if I sell the books and pay back a little maybe they'll give me more time."

Phyllis thought for a minute. "How do you owe so much just to start that shop?"

Peters looked more and more defeated as he spoke. "I owed money when we left Boston. When we lived on Queen Street people thought we had money and didn't push me for it so much. Now that we've come back . . . and the war . . . well they want to be paid."

"Did you owe money before we were married?"

"Yes," Peters nodded.

Phyllis turned from her husband. Again, she could hear Obdour's words. She had trusted Peters. She had tried to give him children. The result was heart-breaking loss for Phyllis. All her efforts to be a good wife seemed foolish to her. What then occurred to her, however, was how she had married Peters because she did not think she was able to take care of herself. His desire to marry her may have been questionable. Hers, however, Phyllis had to admit, was as well. She walked to the little table in the corner of the room where they were standing and gathered her books. As she did so, she held her volume of Alexander Pope and the copy of Milton's Paradise Lost gently, as if they were delicate objects of art. These books, and the others, were the only things left to her from a life that had been magical. Now, they would be forfeit. Phyllis returned to her husband and gave him her treasures. As she placed them in his hands, Phyllis saw that he had no idea how much she was sacrificing. Peters could read, but never picked up a book. To him, these were simply objects, worth enough, he hoped, to buy him a few more days of freedom. As he took the books, however, Phyllis could see that her husband was not through with his expectations.

"What else, John?"

John Peters looked at his wife. He well knew what her reaction might be to his next request. "I want you to publish another book of your poems."

Phyllis stared at her husband. She pinched her eyes as if trying to look through a crack in a fence. Her husband had never shown any interest in her writing. She was certain that he had not bothered to look at her first collection of poems, even though she kept a copy on a table everywhere they had lived. That book meant more to her than she would have been able to explain. Only her copy of her Bible was more precious. To her husband, however, it had seemed to be nothing more than an object of decoration. He had bragged of her literary reputation when speaking with someone he hoped to impress. That was what her poetry meant to him. And certainly, he had never encouraged her to continue her writing after they were married.

"I can give you some of the money from selling your books. You can use it to put a notice in the newspapers."

"I can't," Phyllis said quietly.

Her husband's shoulders sank. "It is the only way I know we can make any money. You wrote one book. You can write another."

"Mrs. Wheatley made plans for my first book. And I don't have poems…"

"I've heard you say that you had poems you didn't put in that first book," John Peters snapped.

"Yes," Phyllis said. "Poems I wrote about things happening here. The English didn't have no use for them I figured."

"Then you can use those poems," Peters said.

"They still won't sell in England."

"Then you sell them here." Her husband's tone was growing increasingly angry, and Phyllis knew that there was little she might say that would make him understand.

"People here don't have money for books. They fighting a war."

"People who read have money. They bought your first book."

Phyllis shook her head. "That was different. They bought it after it had been sold in London."

John Peters turned from his wife and walked back to the stove where he again added a piece of wood and held his hands out to soak up the warmth. Phyllis moved as well and took a seat as far from him as she could get. Her husband had never cared about her writing, and now he was insisting that she prepare another work. She was again carrying a child. Her health was poor and not likely to improve considering the poor food and living conditions they endured. All the people who had helped her before when she published her poems were gone. She would enjoy neither their encouragement nor their practical advice. No wonder he can't make a business work, Phyllis thought. He doesn't understand how things are. He was all ideas, but nothing else.

"I can't, John. I wish I could."

Peters turned on his wife. "You have to. It's the only thing I know for us to do."

"John…

"They will put me in debtors' prison."

"You said that was why you needed to sell my books. To keep you out of prison."

"It isn't going to be enough," Peters said. "I owe too much money. If we sell your books. And if you do a notice, and I give them a little money . . . maybe they can wait on the rest. If they see we are going to do something."

Phyllis stared at the panicked look in her husband's eyes. She had seen the look before. Years ago. It was the look of Africans right after they had been taken into slavery. It was they look in their eyes the first time they saw the ocean and had been terrified by its size. It was the look of men and women waiting in line to be branded with the sign of their owner. It was the look that had been in her eyes as she sat on the docks of Boston harbor as strange men and women walked around her trying to decide which of the Negroes to purchase. All these years Phyllis had lived comfortably she had not again seen that same look of fear. But there it was, in the eyes of the man she had married. John Peters feared that he was about to lose his freedom.

"I'll try," Phyllis whispered.

The smile her husband gave her was not one of joy, but rather relief. Phyllis could not offer a similar response. She slumped in the chair and placed her hands on her stomach which was only just beginning to swell with the child she was carrying. In that moment, she realized that she was not going to try to sell a book because of the joy it would bring her. Nor was she going to make the effort for her husband. Phyllis was not going to write poetry for the love of writing. She was going to do it because it was the only thing she could do to try to provide for the child that she would give birth to in a few months.

* * *

John Peters' fortunes did not improve. He was unable to avoid the price of his business efforts failing and his trying to avoid people whom he owed money. Finally, he was placed in debtors' prison. As a result, Phyllis was left on her own. In desperate need of money, she did return to her one great skill, her writing. Between October and December 1779, Phyllis ran six advertisements seeking buyers for a second book of her poetry which she indicated she would dedicate to Benjamin Franklin. Her proposed book was to be a 300-page octavo edition containing thirty-three new poems and thirteen letters. Phyllis set the price at twelve pounds for a leather bound edition, or nine pounds for a sewn copy. America was a war-poor nation, however. Even the dedication to such a famous patriot as Franklin did not help her efforts. She was unable to find sufficient support to convince a printer to take on the project. This volume would have contained Phyllis' America poems, so her English audience which had bought the first volume would now be lost to her.

With her husband in debtors' prison and her poetry not finding an audience, Phyllis took a job as a scullery maid and charwoman in a Negro boarding house. She had given birth to two children. Both were born frail and did not live long. Nor was Phyllis physically suited to the work she was able to find. She had been a sickly child when John and Susanna Wheatley had bought her. She had never been required, or even permitted, to do serious household chores in their home. Phyllis Wheatley was so poorly prepared for the life that she was forced to live that her own health failed. On December 5, 1784, shortly after the birth of a third child, Phyllis Wheatley died. The child followed within hours. Both were buried in an unmarked grave in Boston. Only the Independent Chronicle noted the passing of the remarkable African poet who had once been the talk of London society. That notice read:

> Last Lord's day died, Mrs. PHYLLIS PETERS, (formerly Phyllis Wheatley) aged 31, known to the literary world by her celebrated miscellaneous Poems. Her funeral is to be this afternoon, at 4 o'clock, from the house lately improved by Mr. Todd, nearly opposite Dr. Bulfinch's, at West-Boston, where her friends and acquaintance(s) are desired to attend.

Shortly after his wife's death, John Peters was released and went to the niece of Susanna Wheatley, Elizabeth Walcutt, with whom Phyllis had left the manuscript of her proposed second book. Peters demanded the material before moving to the South where he faded into history. The manuscript was lost as well and with it many of Phyllis' poems.

Chapter VI

Phyllis Wheatley and Slavery

Several times during her life, friends of Phyllis Wheatley tried to convince her to take an active role in the Abolitionist movement. She never did, nor did she very often voice her thoughts about the slavery question. Much of what she did say actually argued against parts of the Abolitionist philosophy, even though her own life pointed out that African Negroes were as smart and creative as whites. So, what did Phyllis Wheatley think about slavery? After all, she had been kidnapped and taken her from her home at a tender age.

At least part of Phyllis' thinking about slavery shows in the poem "On Being Brought from Africa to America":

'Twas mercy brought me from my Pagan land,
Taught my benighted soul to understand
That there's a God, that there's a Saviour too:
Once I redemption neither sought nor knew.
Some view our sable race with scornful eye
"Their colour is diabolic die."
Remember, Christians, Negros, black as Cain,
May be refin'd, and join th' angelic train.

This short poem contains two important ideas. The first is Phyllis' statement that by being taken as a slave she was able to live in a Christian country and receive salvation. Cotton Mather said much the same thing in 1693 in his work *Rules for the Society of the Negroes*. On the other hand, Phyllis' poem does remind whites that Africans are also the children of God. She would have heard this idea expressed by Reverend Whitefield at the Old South Church.

A stronger statement about slavery appears in Phyllis' February 11, 1774, letter to Reverend Samson Occom, a Mohegan Indian and Christian missionary. In the letter, she compares the enslavement of Africans with the Egyptian enslavement of the Hebrews. In that letter, Phyllis stated, "God grant deliverance in his own way and time, and get him honour upon all those whose avarice impels them to countenance and help the calamities of their fellow creatures." Perhaps had Phyllis been bought by someone other than John Wheatley or had a mistress more demanding than Susanna, she would have been more willing to strongly criticize slavery. On the other hand, had Phyllis Wheatley been treated as a typical slave, she would never have learned to read, written poetry, or been in a position to have her thoughts on any subject considered important.

Phyllis Wheatley's decision not to take an active role in the Abolitionist movement may have frustrated many of her admirers. Certainly John Thornton had been disappointed when Phyllis decided against going to Africa as a Christian missionary. Granville Sharp had almost despaired that Phyllis had not claimed her freedom when she landed in London. All three decisions, however, typified Phyllis' life. She cared very much for the causes of freedom and Christian salvation. She simply chose to fight for those causes through her writing. The result was that Phyllis Wheatley proved by example that Africans brought to America could be and deserved to be viewed as equal participants in the emerging American dream. In the 1830s, more than a hundred years after Phyllis' passing, Abolitionists printed her poems in an effort to confront the belief in the inherent inferiority of Negroes. Long after her death, Phyllis Wheatley finally joined the cause which she supported best by simply being what she had been created, a woman of intelligence and creativity.

Terms and Names to Know

Senegambia—The region of West Africa surrounding the Gambia River which today comprises the two countries of Gambia and Senegal. During the eighteenth and nineteenth century, this part of Africa was at the center of the slave trade.

coffle—In the slave trade, a coffle was a column of slaves tied or shackled together used to keep captured Africans together during marches from the inland to the coast.

barracoon—In the slave trade, a barracoon was an enclosed area in which slaves were kept while waiting to be sold or traded to Europeans for transport to the West Indies or American colonies.

Middle Passage—This notorious term was used to refer to the second part of the three-part journey of a slave ship. The first part was the trip from Europe to Africa when the ships carried goods to trade for slaves. The third part was the trip from the West Indies or American colonies containing tobacco, sugar, rum, and other products much desired in Europe. The second part, referred to as the Middle Passage, was the journey transporting slaves, often under inhuman conditions, from Africa to the west.

Abolitionist—The social and political movement devoted to ending slavery in all its forms.

University of Cambridge—Later know as Harvard University.

George Whitefiled—Distinguished member of the clergy and chaplain to the Countess of Huntingdon, Whitefield was a central figure in what was know as the Great Awakening.

Great Awakening—An evangelical movement in America during the eighteenth century when many in the clergy felt that the colonists had become excessively concerned with practical and political matters and turned away from religion. These clergy attempted to initiate an American revival of religious commitment.

Selina Hastings, Countess of Huntingdon—An important figure in the Abolitionist struggle in England and extremely religious person, Hastings' support of Phyllis Wheatley was crucial to the success of the poet's career.

British Blockade—After the Boston Tea Party, December 16, 1773, the British sent warships to close off the harbor cities crucial to commerce in the American colonies.

octavo volume—A book composed of sheets of paper folded three times, creating eight leaves or sixteen pages.

John Paul Jones—Famous American naval captain noted for his statement "I have not yet begun to fight."

manumission—the legal emancipation of an individual slave.

mackroon—A term used to refer to sick or dying captured Africans who were deemed unsuitable for shipment to the colonies and who were killed in order to preserve food and prevent the spread of disease to other slaves.

Boston Massacre—On March 5, 1770, a mob of Bostonians harassing a British sentry were fired upon, killing five persons in the crowd.

Thomas Paine—A leading figure in the American Revolution, Paine's Common Sense (1776) urged the colonists to declare their independence.

Cotton Mather—A member of the prominent Puritan Mather family, his conservative beliefs contributed to the witch hysteria in colonial New England.

Important Dates

1761—In the spring of this year, Phyllis Wheatley was adducted from her home in Senegambia, West Africa, taken to Boston, and sold to John and Susanna Wheatley.

1767—Phyllis' first published poem, "On Messrs. Hussey and Coffin," appears in the *Newport Mercury.*

1770—Phyllis attends sermons delivered by George Whitefield and then becomes a member of the Old South Church in Boston.

1771—Phyllis is baptized by Reverend Dr. Samuel Cooper.

1771—Phyllis' poem "On the Death of the Rev'd Mr. George Whitefield—1770" published as a broadside.

1772—Susanna Wheatley advertises a proposed volume of Phyllis' poems but does not find adequate interest to publish the work in America.

1773—On May 8, Phyllis leaves Boston to supervise the completion of her book in London, but returns after a brief stay to attend to the ailing Susanna Wheatley, arriving back in Boston at the end of July.

1773—In June, Phyllis' book, *Poems on Various Subjects, Religious and Moral*, appears in London.

1774—Phyllis' book available in New England and Novia Scotia.

1774—In January, Phyllis is freed by John Wheatley.

1774—On March 3, Susanna Wheatley dies, leaving Phyllis feeling as if she has lost a member of her own family.

1776—Phyllis has brief meeting with George Washington at the General's Cambridge headquarters.

1778—John Wheatley and Mary Wheatley Lathrop both die.

1778—April 1, Phyllis marries John Peters.

1779—Phyllis attempts to publish a second volume of poems and letters, but cannot find sufficient support.

1783—Nathaniel Wheatley dies in London.

1784—Phyllis Wheatley and her third, and last child, die in Boston and are buried in an unmarked grave.

Bibliography

Carretta, Vincent, ed. *Phyllis Wheatley: Complete Writings*. New York: Penguin Books, 2001.

Gates, Henry Louis, Jr. *The Trials of Phyllis Wheatley: America's First Black Poet and Her Encounters with the Founding Fathers*. New York: Basic Books, 2003.

Graham, Shirley. *The Story of Phyllis Wheatley*. New York: J. Messner, 1949.

Gregson, Susan R. *Let Freedom Ring: Phyllis Wheatley*. Mankato, Minnesota: Bridgestone Books, 2002.

Mason, Julian. *Poems of Phyllis Wheatley*. Chapel Hill: University of North Carolina Press, 1966.

Richmond, Merle. *Phyllis Wheatley*. American Women of Achievement Series. New York: Chelsea House, 1988.

Rinaldi, Ann. *Hang a Thousand Trees with Ribbons: The Story of Phyllis Wheatley*. New York: Gulliver Books, Inc., 1996.

Robinson, William H. *Phyllis Wheatley: A Bio-Biography*. Boston: G.K. Hall, 1981.

_____. *Phyllis Wheatley in the Black American Beginnings*. Detroit: Broadside Publishing, 1975.

_____. *Phyllis Wheatley and Her Writings*. New York: Garland Publishing, Inc., 1984.

Salisbury, Cynthia. *Phyllis Wheatley: Legendary African-American Poet*. Berkeley Heights, New Jersey: Enslow Publishers, Inc., 2001.

Schneider, Dorothy and Carl J. Schneider. *An Eyewitness History of Slavery in America: From Colonial Times to the Civil War*. New York: Checkmark Books, 2001.

Shields, John C., ed. *The Collected Works of Phyllis Wheatley*. New York: Oxford University Press, 1989.

Thatcher, B. B. *Memoir of Phyllis Wheatley, A Native African and a Slave*. New York: Moore and Payne, 1834.

Weidt, Maryann N. *Revolutionary Poet: A Story about Phyllis Wheatley*. Minneapolis: Carolrhoda Books, Inc., 1997.

Printed in the United States
152463LV00011B/194/P